KU-606-622

The Trouble with Maths

A practical guide to helping learners
with numeracy difficulties

Steve Chinn

 RoutledgeFalmer
Taylor & Francis Group

LONDON AND NEW YORK

First published 2004 by RoutledgeFalmer
2 Park Square, Milton Park, Abingdon, Oxon OX14 4RN

Simultaneously published in the USA and Canada
by RoutledgeFalmer
270 Madison Ave, New York, NY 10016

Reprinted with text corrections 2005 (twice)

Transferred to Digital Printing 2007

RoutledgeFalmer is an imprint of the Taylor & Francis Group, an informa business

© 2004 Steve Chinn

Typeset in Times New Roman and Gill Sans by
Florence Production Ltd, Stoodleigh, Devon
Printed and bound in Great Britain

All rights reserved. No part of this book may be reprinted or
reproduced in any form or by any electronic, mechanical,
or other means, now known or hereafter invented, including
photocopying and recording, or in any information storage
or retrieval system, without permission in writing from
the publishers.

British Library Cataloguing in Publication Data
A catalogue record for this book is available from the
British Library

Library of Congress Cataloging in Publication Data
A catalogue record has been requested

ISBN 10: 0-415-32498-X
ISBN 13: 978-0-415-32498-4

Contents

Illustrations

Figures

Tables

Foreword

For many years, the field of children's learning difficulties has been dominated by research on reading and dyslexia. There is now a large body of knowledge concerning the nature and origins of dyslexia and how best to teach reading to children with such difficulties. However, learning to read is not the only skill that poses difficulty for children with dyslexia-related disorders – the majority also have difficulty with at least some aspects of number work. 'The Trouble with Maths' addresses this issue and shows how all who teach and learn maths can enjoy it.

Scientific research on number skills has increased during the past ten years and the evidence base is growing at a rapid rate. It is now known that, from shortly after birth, infants can detect changes in the number of objects in visual displays of objects. This innate sense of numerosity is the foundation of later number concepts that develop rapidly during the pre-school years. But to become numerate demands more; children need to learn conventional systems and to use their mathematical thinking meaningfully and flexibly in logical situations. Neuroscientists mapping brain-behaviour relationships have shown that mathematical expertise draws on a wide range of neural circuits in the right and left hemispheres that must work in concert to solve mathematical problems. It is therefore not surprising, as Steve Chinn points out, that children's problems with numeracy are diverse and the term 'dyscalculia' may be too broad to capture the wide range of problems that are observed in children acquiring mathematical skills.

At the broadest level, numeracy problems may affect either mathematical thinking or computational skills. But during development, as this book shows, the situation is never quite so simple; mathematical learning is a cumulative process so that a poorly developed concept of number can affect the acquisition of number facts and by the same token, poor arithmetic ability can compromise the growth of mathematical knowledge. Furthermore, school mathematics is embedded in language, requires sequencing skills, draws on working memory systems, depends on spatial concepts and, more than any other school subject, engenders anxiety. Add to this the fact that the assessment of mathematical learning usually requires the child to read and comprehend written questions and to lay out their work clearly, and the whole area become a minefield for the child with specific learning difficulties.

Steve Chinn has done a great job of systemising what can be done to help the child who has problems with maths. His message is clear – take account of the strengths of the child and the style of their thinking, marry this with the demands of the numeracy curriculum and adjust lessons to help. The book shows how careful assessment can lead to the development of effective strategies to help with basic and more advanced concepts of maths. There is discussion of what data mathematics tests can provide (and by inference what they cannot) and a checklist for choosing assessment instruments. There are heaps of ideas for successful teaching and advice on both how to set up an individual education plan and how to develop an inclusive mathematics curriculum.

Written from the perspective of a highly skilled practitioner and an expert teacher-educator who enjoys and understands numbers, this book ensures that all who read it will understand how to teach maths in such a way that every child can achieve their potential.

Maggie Snowling
University of York
February 2004

Chapter 1

Introduction
Learning difficulties in mathematics

This book is to help teachers, classroom assistants and learning support assistants who have to deal with pupils who are underachieving in mathematics. It takes several perspectives on the situation, from preventive measures to diagnosis and identification of difficulties, to thinking styles, to ideas for intervention. It works like a repair manual in some respects and like a care awareness manual (looking after your students) in other respects.

It is a book which can be accessed in different ways. It can provide an overview of where and how problems may arise. It offers insights into areas of potential difficulty. It can focus on a particular problem and suggest approaches which can help the pupil to learn, but it would be an impossible task to attempt to provide an answer for every problem for every child.

It can be used to:

◆ identify a problem
◆ understand possible reasons for a problem
◆ pre-empt problems
◆ develop flexible thinking skills
◆ circumvent problems in basic numeracy
◆ address the difficulties pupils have with word problems
◆ teach alternative strategies for accessing basic facts
◆ recognise maths anxiety, attributional style and self-esteem problems
◆ design informal diagnostic procedures
◆ extract diagnostic information from pupils' work
◆ stimulate ideas for teaching maths to pupils who are facing difficulties with the subject.

Sometimes you may find information repeated in different chapters of the book. This is deliberate as some observations fit into more than one area. The new area should give a different perspective to that information.

What do learners need to be good at mathematics?

Although this book is about what to do when learners are underachieving in maths, it should be valuable to consider what learners need to be good at maths. I have two sources for this information. One is from the USSR and the other from the USA.

Krutetskii[1] presented a broad outline of the structure of mathematical abilities during school age. He specifies:

♦ The ability for logical thought in the sphere of quantitative and spatial relationships, number and letter symbols; the ability to think in mathematical symbols.
♦ The ability for rapid and broad generalisation of mathematical objects, relations and operations.
♦ Flexibility of mental processes in mathematical activity.
♦ Striving for clarity, simplicity, economy and rationality of solutions.
♦ The ability for rapid and free reconstruction of the direction of a mental process, switching from a direct to a reverse train of thought.
♦ Mathematical memory (generalised memory for mathematical relationships), and for methods of problem solving and principles of approach.
♦ These components are closely interrelated, influencing one another and forming in their aggregate a single integral syndrome of mathematical giftedness.

Although Krutetskii makes these observations concerning giftedness in mathematics, they are equally appropriate for competence. The reader can see where learning difficulties may create problems.

The other source is the National Council of Teachers of Mathematics in the USA, who list and explain twelve essential components of essential maths:

1 *Problem solving* The process of applying previously acquired knowledge to new and unfamiliar situations. Students should see alternate solutions to problems: they should experience problems with more than a single solution.

2 *Communicating mathematical ideas (receiving and presenting)* Students should learn the language and notation of maths.

3 *Mathematical reasoning* Students should learn to make independent investigations of mathematical ideas. They should be able to identify and extend patterns and use experiences and observations to make conjectures.

4 *Applying maths to everyday situations* Students should be encouraged to take everyday situations, translate them into mathematical representations (graphs, tables, diagrams or mathematical expressions), process the maths and interpret the results in light of the initial situation.

5 *Alertness to the reasonableness of results* In solving problems, students should question the reasonableness of a solution or conjecture in relation to the original problem. They must develop number sense.

6 *Estimation* Students should be able to carry out rapid approximate calculations through the use of mental arithmetic and a variety of computational estimation techniques and decide when a particular result is precise enough for the purpose in hand.

7 *Appropriate computational skills*   Students should gain facility in using addition, subtraction, multiplication and division with whole numbers and decimals. Today long complicated computations should be done with a calculator or a computer. Knowledge of single digit number facts is essential.

8 *Algebraic thinking*   Students should learn to use variables (letters) to represent mathematical quantities and expressions. They should understand and use correctly positive and negative numbers, order of operations, formulas, equations and inequalities.

9 *Measurement*   Students should learn the fundamental concepts of measurement through concrete experiences.

10 *Geometry*   Students should understand the geometric concepts necessary to function effectively in the three dimensional world.

11 *Statistics*   Students should plan and carry out the collection and organisation of data to answer questions in their everyday lives. Students should recognise the basic uses and misuses of statistical representation and inference.

12 *Probability*   Students should understand the elementary notions of probability to determine the likelihood of future events. They should learn how probability applies to the decision making process.

And, picking up on Krutetskii's first point concerning the use of symbols in maths, the British psychologist, Skemp[2] wrote:

Among the functions of symbols, we can distinguish:

(1) Communication
(2) Recording knowledge
(3) The communication of new concepts
(4) Making multiple classification straightforward
(5) Explanations
(6) Making possible reflective activity
(7) Helping to show structure
(8) Making routine manipulations automatic
(9) Recovering information and understanding
(10) Creative mental activity.

He concludes that: 'It is largely by the use of symbols that we achieve voluntary control over our thoughts.'

So, we have some characteristics for being good at mathematics. Could one assume that deficits in all or some of these skills create difficulties in mathematics? I know from experience that there are many reasons why someone may underachieve in mathematics and that the picture is a complex one with no single root cause. Recently the term dyscalculia has become more prominent and so a look at what dyscalculia might be may help our understanding of other reasons for difficulties with mathematics.

Dyscalculia, definitions and descriptions

Dyscalculia, a problem with learning mathematics, is attracting attention in official circles. The DfES (Department for Education and Skills) has published a booklet (see end of chapter) on guidance for supporting pupils with dyscalculia (and dyslexia) in the National Numeracy Strategy (NNS). There is now a screening test for dyscalculia (Butterworth 2003) published by NFER-Nelson. Despite this attention the literature on dyscalculia is sparse and the definitions are a little bland at present. I have extracted a few from various sources.

Developmental dyscalculia is defined by Bakwin and Bakwin (1960) as a 'difficulty with counting' and by Cohn (1968) as a 'failure to recognise numbers or manipulate them in an advanced culture'. Gerstmann (1957) describes dyscalculia (Gerstmann's syndrome) as 'an isolated disability to perform simple or complex arithmetical operations and an impairment of orientation in the sequence of numbers and their fractions.'

Kosc (1974) describes developmental dyscalculia as a structural disorder of mathematical abilities which has its origin in a genetic or congenital disorder of those parts of the brain that are the direct anatomico-physiological substrate of the maturation of the mathematical abilities adequate to age, without a simultaneous disorder of general mental functions. This definition clearly puts dyscalculia in the inherited and specific learning difficulties category.

In 1996 Magne gave a slightly more cautious explanation of a difficulty in mathematics as the low achievement of a person on a certain occasion which manifests itself as performance below standard of the age-group of this person or below his own abilities as a consequence of inadequate cognitive, affective, volitional, motor or sensory etc. development. The cause for inadequate development may be of various kinds. This description acknowledges that there will be more than one cause for difficulties in mathematics.

Mahesh Sharma (1986) lists the many words that have been suggested for maths difficulties, explaining terms such as acalculia, dyscalculia, anarithmetica and noting that there is no definite agreement on their use universally in the literature, that they have not been used consistently, and although there are significant differences between dyscalculia and acalculia, some authors have used the terms interchangeably. He concludes that the descriptions of these terms are quite diverse to say the least.

Sharma suggests that dyscalculia refers to a disorder in the ability to do or to learn mathematics, that is, difficulty in number conceptualisation, understanding number relationships and difficulty in learning algorithms and applying them. It is an irregular impairment of ability. Thus Sharma suggests that dyscalculia is a specific learning difficulty.

Acalculia is used to label a more serious condition, the loss of the fundamental processes of quantity and magnitude estimation and a complete loss of the ability to count. This is an acquired condition.

And, finally, something that sounds like a missing member of the Russian royal family, arithmastenia, defined as a uniform deficiency in the level of mathematical abilities.

I wrote the following for the Dyslexia Institute's journal, *Dyslexia Review*, volume 14, number 3, 2003. It is reprinted with their permission.

Does dyscalculia add up?

Initial ramblings

Is dyscalculia 'dyslexia with maths'?

With the publication of Brian Butterworth's *The Dyscalculia Screener* and the inclusion of dyscalculia as a specific learning difficulty in the DfES consultation document for the 2004 SEN census, dyscalculia is a hot topic. This article sums (!) up my current thinking about dyscalculia. Unfortunately my current thinking is fluid. I am trying to make sense of all those factors which influence the maths learning outcomes of children and adults. So, I hope this paper may attract some responses and stimulate more research.

Since absolute knowledge on dyscalculia is in short supply I am going to construct this paper around the questions which I consider we have to investigate to reach an understanding of dyscalculia. In doing this there seem to be some very interesting comparisons between dyscalculia and dyslexia.

There are some things I know as a start. I know that dyscalculia will not be a simple construct (I think that means a psychological concept). I know that there will be many reasons why a person may be bad at maths. I know there will not be any instant or simple 'cures' because I know that there is unlikely to be a single reason behind the problem of the many, many people who fail to master maths and I know that not all of these will be dyscalculic.

I heard David Geary speak at the last IDA conference. This American guru compared our knowledge of dyslexia to being close to adulthood and our knowledge of maths/dyscalculia to being in its early infancy. This is reflected in the number of research studies done on language difficulties compared to those done on maths difficulties. As for studies on dyscalculia, they are few indeed. I think there are so many parallels at so many levels between dyslexia and dyscalculia and all that surrounds these specific learning difficulties, for example prevalence, definition, teaching methods, etiology and so forth.

We are some twenty years behind language/dyslexia studies in our knowledge and understanding of dyscalculia. This is not to say that I think it will take us twenty years to catch up in all areas, but that it takes a good length of time for the concept to become accepted in everyday educational settings and thus for understandings to build from work from the 'shop floor'.

So, let's go back twenty years to a much quoted, pioneering paper by Joffe (1980). One of Joffe's statistics has been applied over-enthusiastically and without careful consideration of how it was obtained. This is the '61 per cent of dyslexics are retarded in arithmetic' and thus 39 per cent are not. Now it is not quite as simple as that. The sample for this statistic was quite small, some 50 dyslexic learners. The maths test on which the statistic was largely based was the British Abilities Scales Basic Arithmetic Test which is just that, a test of arithmetic skills. Although the test was untimed, Joffe noted that the high attainment group would have done less well if speed was a consideration. The extrapolations from this paper would have to be cautious. Other writers seem to have overlooked Joffe's own cautious and detailed observations, for example, 'Computation was a slow and laborious process for a large proportion of the dyslexic sample.' You will see at the very end of this paper I have mentioned a Mark College pupil who was identified as dyscalculic by the Butterworth screener (where two out of the five exercises focus on speed and accuracy in computation) but who is predicted to achieve a Grade A in GCSE maths.

I think there are two reasons why Joffe's paper is so frequently quoted. One is that it is a good paper and the other is that there are so few others from which to quote. NFER-Nelson describe Brian Butterworth as 'the leading expert on dyscalculia'. Sadly, at the moment it's a one horse race. We need more researchers to follow Butterworth's initiative.

Definitions and labels

As a (lapsed) physicist I have a scientist's concept of what makes a definition. In physics one can control the variables and do pretty reliable experiments. People are difficult to control (especially as teenagers). In this respect I view some definitions as descriptions.

The definition of a learning difficulty can be very influential and can have many consequences. For example, it can influence the allocation of resources to an individual or to a school or to the education budget of an Education Authority. For an individual, knowing that your difficulties have a label may be a relief and a benefit, but it may also cause a reaction not at all dissimilar to that of grieving for a loss. So there needs to be a sense of responsibility and awareness of all these implications in those who create definitions.

There seems to have been a change in the culture of the definition of dyslexia, from the all encompassing definitions of the late 80s to the focused, minimalist definition of the British Psychological Society in the late 90s. This could well be significant. Professor Tim Miles talks of 'lumpers' and 'splitters'. So, could there be 'specific learning difficulties' which may encompass all or some of dyslexia, dyspraxia and dyscalculia or can the three dys's have independent existences?

Does being dyscalculic exclude you from being dyslexic or dyspraxic? Does being dyslexic exclude you from being dyscalculic? Then, turning to the lumpers, does being dyslexic mean you are also dyscalculic and dyspraxic?

It may help to answer some, if not all of these questions if you think of real people, real individuals and what the answer would be for Jeff or Jane. My feeling is that the answer to the first two questions is 'No' and to the third question, 'Not necessarily.'

Of course the answers depend on the definitions currently assigned to the difficulties. I'll come back to summarise my thoughts on definitions towards the end of this paper, but here is a small sample of definitions for now.

The first is from a DfES booklet (2001) on supporting pupils with dyslexia and dyscalculia in the NNS.

Dyscalculia is a condition that affects the ability to acquire mathematical skills. Dyscalculic learners may have difficulty understanding simple number concepts, lack an intuitive grasp of numbers, and have problems learning number facts and procedures. Even if they produce a correct answer or use a correct method, they may do so mechanically and without confidence.

Very little is known about the prevalence of dyscalculia, its causes, or treatment. Purely dyscalculic learners who have difficulties only with numbers will have cognitive and language abilities in the normal range, and may excel in non-mathematical subjects. It is more likely that difficulties with numeracy accompany the language difficulties of dyslexia.

The second dates from 1970 and is attributed to Kosc (1974).

Developmental dyscalculia is a structural disorder of mathematical abilities which has its origin in a genetic or congenital disorder of those parts of the brain that are the direct anatomico-physiological substrate of the maturation of the mathematical abilities adequate to age, without a simultaneous disorder of general mental functions.

Sharma (1990) discusses three terms for difficulties in mathematics, saying that,

Terms such as acalculia, dyscalculia, anarithmetica . . . there is no definite agreement on their use universally in the literature . . . they have not been used consistently . . . although there are significant differences between dyscalculia and acalculia, some authors have used the terms interchangeably . . . the descriptions of these terms are quite diverse to say the least.

He explains dyscalculia and acalculia as:

Dyscalculia refers to a disorder in the ability to do or to learn mathematics, that is, difficulty in number conceptualisation, understanding number relationships and difficulty in learning algorithms and applying them. (An irregular impairment of ability).

Acalculia is the loss of fundamental processes of quantity and magnitude estimation. (A complete loss of the ability to count.)

The final example is from a DfES consultation document called 'Classification of SEN.' The descriptions are to be used in the pupil level annual schools census from 2004 (DfES 2002).

Specific learning difficulty (SpLD) covers a range of related conditions which occur across a continuum of severity. Pupils may have difficulties in reading, writing, spelling or manipulating numbers which are not typical of their general level of performance. Pupils may have difficulty with short-term memory, with organisational skills, with hand–eye co-ordination and with orientation and directional awareness. Dyslexia, dyscalculia and dyspraxia fall under this umbrella.

Pupils with dyscalculia have difficulty with numbers and remembering mathematical facts as well as performing mathematical operations. Pupils may have difficulties with abstract concepts of time and direction, recalling schedules and sequences of events as well as difficulties with mathematical concepts, rules, formulas and basic addition, subtraction, multiplication and division of facts.

What distinguishes dyscalculia from just problems with maths? What do we mean by 'problems with maths'? How big is the problem?

We don't know. It will depend on the definition. It may also depend on the perseverance of the difficulty. Goodness knows how many people have a 'difficulty' with maths. Like all skills, if you cease to practise you lose the skill and few adults practise maths, especially topics such as fractions or algebra, after leaving school. So the extent of the problem could well increase in adults. For example, a study done in 1995 on behalf of the Basic Skills Agency of 1714 adults aged 35 years found that just under one quarter had very low numeracy skills at a level which would make it difficult to complete everyday tasks successfully.

So I am sure that just having a difficulty with maths should not automatically earn you the label 'dyscalculic'.

Dyscalculia introduces another word into the vocabulary of special needs. Some see these words as labels and thus as descriptors of a person. That would not be helpful.

OK, I'm dyscalculic. So what?

I like the questions, 'What if?' and the follow up 'So what?' 'What if I am dyscalculic, so what?' I have to ask does being dyscalculic condemn the learner to being forever unsuccessful at maths. That then raises further questions:

'What does it mean to be successful at maths?' and 'What skills and strengths does a learner need to be successful at maths?' and 'Is it important to be successful at maths?'

At my school, Mark College, a DfES approved independent school for boys who have been diagnosed as dyslexic, the results for GCSE maths are significantly above national average. Usually at least 75 per cent of grades are at C and above compared to the national average of around 50 per cent. Obviously I believe that if the teaching is appropriate then a learning difficulty does not necessarily mean lack of achievement. But, does a C grade or above in GCSE maths define success? That's a question for another article, so, for the purpose of this article let's assume it is one criterion and let's assume this is one piece of evidence that appropriate teaching can make a difference.

As for maths, well there is the maths you need for everyday life. This rarely includes algebra, fractions (other than $\frac{1}{4}$ and $\frac{1}{2}$), co-ordinates or indeed much of what is taught in secondary schools. It does include a lot of money, measurement, some time and the occasional percentage. Take, as an example of a real life maths exercise, paying for a family meal in a restaurant. It needs estimation skills, possibly accurate addition skills, subtraction skills if using cash, and percentage skills for the tip.

The Russian psychologist Krutetskii (1976) listed the components of mathematical ability which could act as a description of what a learner needs to be 'good at maths' and thus also act as a guide as to what may be the deficits which handicap the learner failing to be good at maths (also listed on page 21ff in more detail).

1   An ability to formalise maths material (to abstract oneself from concrete numerical relationships).
2   An ability to generalise and abstract oneself from the irrelevant.
3   An ability to operate with numerals and other symbols.
4   An ability for sequential segmented logical reasoning.
5   An ability to shorten the reasoning process.
6   An ability to reverse a mental process.
7   Flexibility of thought.
8   A mathematical memory.
9   An ability for spatial concepts.

What is maths?

Could a person be good at some bits of maths and a failure at other bits? Do you have to fail at ALL bits to be dyscalculic?

In terms of subject content, early maths is mostly numbers. Later it becomes more varied with new topics introduced such as measure, algebra and spatial topics. Up to GCSE, despite the different headings, the major component remains as number. So the demands of maths can appear quite broad, and this can be very useful, but number can be a disproportionate part of early learning experiences.

So poor number skills could be a key factor in dyscalculia. This might suggest that we have to consider the match between the demands of the task and the skills of the learner.

In terms of approach, maths can be a written subject or a mental exercise. It can be formulaic or it can be intuitive. It can be learnt and communicated in either way, or combination of ways by the learner and it can be taught and communicated in either way or combination of ways by the teacher.

Maths can be concrete, but fairly quickly moves to the abstract and symbolic. It has many rules and a surprising number of inconsistencies.

In terms of judgement, feedback and appraisal, maths is quite unique as a school subject. Work is usually a blunt 'right' or 'wrong' and it has to be done quickly.

Even on this brief overview it is obvious that the demands of maths are varied. The importance placed on speed of working could also be another key issue for learners.

Attitude and the affective domain

I don't have the reference, but there was a study done in Scandinavia which summed up the influences of language and maths skills on life. Excuse me if I state the influences somewhat starkly. It is important to remember that people do not have to follow the conclusions of statistical analysis. Being good at English does not predict success in life. Being bad at English predicts failure. Being bad at maths does not predict failure. Being good at maths predicts success.

Of course we all know that being bad at maths holds no social stigma in Western culture. Indeed it may well attract much mutual empathy. So the consequences of dyscalculia are going to have a better social acceptance than the consequences of dyslexia. (For example, I recently read a letter to the *Times* about a restaurant menu, complaining that since it had spelling mistakes the writer would not be eating there. That makes sense).

Schools, of course rarely reflect life. In school there may well be significant consequences of being bad at maths, for example the allocation of the learner to a teaching group which may limit the levels of work in several other subjects. Also in school, unlike life, it's hard to avoid the stuff you don't like or the work you feel you can't do.

Two key factors which aid learning are ability and attitude. The latter can go a long way towards compensating for the former, but then the two factors are pretty closely interlinked, for example when success encourages good attitude.

Some learners just feel that they can't do maths. This may well be a consequence of early unsuccessful learning experiences or feedback which is seen as negative. The judgemental nature of maths, together with the culture of having to do maths quickly can lead children to avoid the risk of being wrong again and again and thus to disassociate themselves from the learning experience (Chinn, 1995). Maths creates anxiety and, sadly it usually seems to be an anxiety that does not facilitate learning. Ashcraft *et al.* (1998) have shown that anxiety in maths can impact on working memory and thus depress performance even more.

Some learners develop an attributional style for maths which makes their attitude personal as in 'I'm too stupid to do maths', pervasive, 'I can't do any maths' and permanent, 'I'll never be able to do maths.' An individual with a combination of those three beliefs could well present as a dyscalculic.

Memory, short, long and not always working

I often pose the question in my lectures 'What does the learner bring?' (to maths). I have already mentioned some factors such as anxiety. But what about memory? I know that Krutetskii (1976) lists mathematical memory as a requirement to be good at maths. I am sure that short term and working memory are vital for mental arithmetic, particularly for those sequential, formula based maths thinkers.

But can a learner compensate for difficulties in some of these requirements and thus 'succeed' in maths?

Now let's go back to school, in England, where we have the excellent National Numeracy Strategy. This truly is, in my opinion an excellent programme, but however excellent the programme, it is virtually impossible to meet the needs of every learner. An essential part of the NNS in the early years of education is mental arithmetic. Now that's an activity that needs memories, long, short and working. So a learner with a poor short term memory could fail maths when it is mental maths, even though he may have the potential to become an effective mathematician. If failure is internalised as a negative attributional style by the learner then that potential may never be realised.

Is Krutetskii's mathematical memory a parallel with Gardner's multiple intelligences? Perhaps there are multiple memories. That would explain some of the discrepancies I have seen in children's memory performances. Like any subject, there is a body of factual information for maths and if a learner can remember and recall this information then he will be greatly advantaged and if he can't . . .

So good memories may be required for doing maths in general. Short term and working memories may be essential for mental maths and mathematical long term memory will be essential for the number facts and formulae you need when doing mental arithmetic.

Counting on and on

The first number test on the Butterworth *Dyscalculia Screener* is for subitizing. This means an ability to look at a random cluster of dots and know how many are there, without counting. Most adults do this at 6 dots plus or minus one.

A person who has to rely entirely on counting for addition and subtraction is severely handicapped in terms of speed and accuracy. Such a person is even more handicapped when trying to use counting for multiplication and division. Often their page is covered in endless tally marks and often they are just lined up, not grouped as ~~1111~~ that is, in fives. Maths is done in counting steps of one. If you show them patterns of dots or groups, they prefer the lines and lines.

It's not just the ability to 'see' and use five. It's the ability to see nine as one less than ten, to see $6 + 5$ as $5 + 5 + 1$, to count on in twos, tens and fives, especially if the pattern is not the basic one of 10, 20, 30 ... but 13, 23, 33, 43 ...

It's the ability to go beyond counting in ones by seeing the patterns and relationships in numbers (Chinn and Ashcroft 1992).

Garden variety or what?

How do we distinguish between a 'garden variety' poor reader and a dyslexic? (Stanovich, 1991) How do we distinguish between a 'garden variety' poor mathematician and a dyscalculic?

I think the answer has a lot to do with perseveration of the difficulty in the face of skilled and varied and appropriate intervention.

Can you be a good reader and still be a dyslexic? Can you be good at some areas of maths and still be dyscalculic? My guess is that the answer to both questions is 'Yes', but for maths it is partly because maths is made up of topics, some of which make quite different demands (and for both questions, good appropriate teaching can make such a difference).

Once again I drift back to problems with numbers as being at the core of dyscalculia. And it is numbers that will prevail in real life, when algebra is just a distant memory. And I guess that the main problem is in accessing these facts accurately and quickly, usually straight from memory, rather than via strategies.

Could there be a parallel between phonics and number facts? For example knowing how to use phonics to spell a word could be compared to using addition facts to add, say, $572 + 319$.

But then not all factors are intellectual. A difficulty may be affected by a bureaucratic decision. Some bureaucrats specify a level of achievement that defines whether or not a child's learning difficulties may be addressed or even assessed, influenced in this decision, at least in part by economic considerations. But, even then, is a child's dyslexia or dyscalculia defined solely by achievement scores? Is there room to consider the individual and what he brings to the situation? Sometimes these decisions are being de-humanised. So, I foresee a child not receiving provision for dyscalculia unless his maths age is five or more years behind the norm, which could mitigate against early intervention for six year old pupils.

Teaching

I claimed that being a physicist influenced the way I think. I am also a teacher and have been for almost 40 years and those years have certainly influenced the way I think, too. The teacher part of my thinking says, among other things, 'So he's dyscalculic, what do you expect me to do next?'

Well, my guess is that using the range of methods and strategies we have developed at Mark College for teaching our dyslexic pupils will also be effective with dyscalculic pupils. Indeed we have probably taught many pupils who have the comorbid problems of dyslexia and dyscalculia. What we address as teachers is the way the pupil presents, not a pupil defined by some stereotypical attributes.

My colleague, Julie Kay when faced with a learner who is struggling with learning maths asks herself the questions, 'Where do I begin? How far back in maths do I go to start the intervention?' This may be a difference, should we need one, between the dyscalculic and the dyslexic who is also bad at maths. It may be that the starting point for the intervention is further back in the curriculum for the dyscalculic than for the dyslexic. Yet another topic to research. It may also be that the subsequent rates of progress are different. Another topic.

And for a final thought in this section, I ask, 'What is the influence of the style of curriculum?' I know, for example, from a European study in which I was involved (Chinn *et al.*, 2001), that the design of the maths curriculum certainly affects thinking style in maths.

So what?

There are many reasons why a child or an adult may fail to learn maths skills and knowledge. For example, a child who finds symbols confusing may have been successful with mental arithmetic, but may find written arithmetic very challenging. There may be other examples of an onset of failure at different times which will most likely depend on the match between the demands of the curriculum and the skills and deficits of the learner, for example, a dyslexic will probably find word problems especially difficult and a child who is not dyslexic, but is learning at the concrete level may find the abstract nature of algebra difficult. A child who is an holistic learner may start to fail in maths if his new teacher uses a sequential and formula based inchworm teaching style. A learner may have a poor mathematical memory and the demands on memory may suddenly exceed his capacity.

A difficulty will depend on the interaction between the demands of the task and the skills and attitudes of the learner. For example, if one of the demands of mental arithmetic is that it be done quickly, then any learner who retrieves and processes facts slowly will have learning difficulties. Learning difficulties are obviously dependent on the learning task.

And none of the underlying contributing factors I have discussed are truly independent. Anxiety, for example is a consequence of many influences. I am hypothesising that the factors I have mentioned are the key ones. There may well be others and the pattern and interactions will vary from individual to individual, but these are my choices for the difficulties at the core of dyscalculia.

Of the definitions I have quoted, I much prefer the NNS version. The DfES consultation paper version seems to describe just difficulties in maths which might occur in anyone. I have added some extra notes into the definition which may then be better seen as a description (and thus not a label).

Dyscalculia is a perseverant condition that affects the ability to acquire mathematical skills despite appropriate instruction. *Dyscalculic learners may have difficulty understanding simple number concepts* (such as place value and use of the four operations, $+$ $-$ $\times$ and $\div$), *lack an intuitive grasp of numbers* (including the value of numbers and understanding and using the inter-relationship of numbers), *and have problems learning, retrieving and using quickly number facts* (for example multiplication tables) *and procedures* (for example long division). *Even if they produce a correct answer or use a correct method, they may do so mechanically and without confidence* (and have no way of knowing or checking that the answer is correct).

The NNS version focuses on number, which makes sense to me. It mentions memory and it includes those who present as competent in some areas, but whose performance has no underlying understanding of number. An addendum could list some of the key contributors, such as:

A learner's difficulties with maths may be exacerbated by anxiety, poor short term memory, inability to use and understand symbols, and inflexible learning style.

Now the definition/description is in this form, it may be possible to set up a diagnostic procedure. That sets another research task and we desperately need more research!

Finally, have I met any learners whom I think would be described accurately as *perseverently and exclusively* dyscalculic? I have, but they were few. I mention two, one is a female, gifted in language (and languages) who had absolutely no idea what '$\frac{1}{2} \times 50$' (presented as symbols) would be. I asked her would the answer be bigger or smaller than 50 and she replied 'Yes'. The other is a male, average at language skills but who could not 'see' that I held out *three* fingers. He had to count them, even as a sixteen year old. He achieved a Grade G in GCSE maths.

There are many others out there who may present as dyscalculic as young learners. It's what happens next that confirms or challenges that description.

To add one piece of evidence to support the 'What happens next' hypothesis, I used Butterworth's The Dyscalculia Screener *on one of our Year 10 students. The Screener diagnosed him as dyscalculic. We are predicting he will achieve an A grade in GCSE maths next year. Are these two statements incompatible? I think the answer lies in the word 'perseverent'.*

If you want to follow up references for this section, they are listed at the end of this chapter.

For me, the main issue here is that not every child or adult who is failing in mathematics is dyscalculic. Even for those who do gain this label, it does not predict an outcome, but it does suggest to me that whatever teaching experiences this dyscalculic pupil has had, they have not been appropriate. I know, from ten years of data on pupils at Mark College, that it is possible for most pupils to change a history of gains in maths age of less than twelve months per year to gains of over twelve months per year, thus moving to 'catch up'. Some of these pupils might have been diagnosed as dyscalculic, some might not. In many senses that was less relevant than their history of underachievement in mathematics.

And would intervention for a dyscalculic be different? The answer is that any difficulty has to be viewed individually, but that the core principles of teaching and learning will probably be drawn from the same compendium of ideas used for dyslexics (see Chinn and Ashcroft 1998).

Adjusting lessons to help pupils who are having difficulties in learning maths

Adjustments to lessons should be based on four principles:

◆ *Empathetic classroom management* which implies an active awareness and consequent adjustment to the learning strengths and difficulties of pupils.
◆ *Responsive flexibility* allows the teacher to have a repertoire of resources and strategies which respond to the individual (and often changing) needs of the pupil.
◆ *Developmental methods* are methods that address the remedial need whilst developing mathematical skills and concepts.
◆ *Effective communication* which infers an awareness of thinking and learning style and an awareness of limitations such as language skills, poor short term memory or slower speeds of working.

The application of these principles should affect all levels of work, from the construction of the syllabus and lesson plans to the setting and marking of homework.

Integrating dyscalculic pupils and other learners who have difficulties with mathematics into the real world of the classroom

1 A structure or programme which builds in regular returns to topics helps learners with poorer long term memories. Frequent revisions and overviews, especially after a short time lapse for reflection help to reinforce learning (largely implicit in the NNS). *The syllabus and programme of work*
2 Programmes that rely heavily on self tuition can allow pupils to develop incorrect procedures and concepts. (I remember the Kent Mathematics Project where pupils worked largely with work cards and at their own pace, but with little or no tuition.)

In the   ✔ Short term memory deficits can affect mental arithmetic skills (which may
classroom   show a marked difference to written arithmetic skills).

✔ Short term memory deficits can affect many other areas of learning such as
  the number of items of instruction a pupil can process at one time. These
  deficits may be auditory or visual or both, so presentation should always
  address both modes.

✔ Look out for short term memory overload (when the pupil will just be over-
  whelmed and recall nothing at all).

✔ If recall of facts (such as times table facts) and procedures (such as subtracting
  from zero) do not become automatic, then there is less mental 'space' left to
  do the main task. This compounds the effect of difficulties. Select 'easy'
  numbers when introducing new arithmetical procedures.

✔ Reading deficits do not affect all areas of mathematics to the same degree and
  are a good example of a deficit that gives rise to a seemingly inexplicable
  change in level of performance (that is, when word problems are introduced).

✔ Some pupils are slower to produce work, due to such factors as writing speed,
  poor organisational skills, finger counting instead of instant recall of facts.
  Speed of working is often an issue in mathematics and can be the cause of
  greatly increased anxiety and greatly decreased levels of performance. Consider
  allowing extra time for tests and examinations. Consider careful selection of
  quantities of work for these pupils.

✔ Anxious learners are often poor risk takers and will not try work they perceive
  to be difficult, thereby avoiding failure (they have usually had enough experience of failure), but they are then not accessing new learning experiences.
  Research in the 1920s showed that a pupil's first experience of applying new
  knowledge is the experience that persists . . . a big problem if he gets that first
  experience wrong. Allow pupils to experiment and fail as one of the steps on
  the path to success, but this has to be a closely controlled strategy.

✔ Some pupils are intuitive, answer-oriented problem solvers who may not learn
  from a step by step, sequentially oriented, formula dependent teacher, and, of
  course, vice versa. There are also significant implications for documentation
  of work. Intuitive workers are usually disinclined to document. These differences in cognitive style (thinking through problems) are present in the whole
  school population, including teachers, but their affect on pupils with dyslexia,
  dyspraxia or dyscalculia (with their other contributing problems) is likely to
  be more critical (see Chapter 4).

✔ Sequential, formula-oriented learners with poor memories are at risk of failure
  in mathematics.

✔ Inaccurate intuitive, answer-oriented learners are at risk.

✔ Dyslexic pupils do not adjust quickly to changes in routine, for example if a
  new teacher expects a different page layout in exercise books.

✔ Consider giving the pupil a times table square to stick into the back of his exercise book (so that he has to make some effort to turn to the information) and make sure he can track successfully to the answers.

✔ Learning is usually more effective if it is presented in a multisensory way. This includes the use of concrete manipulatives, which are often phased out as being 'too young' for secondary pupils. Manipulatives may be used as demonstrations, using overhead projector materials or via PC and boards. This avoids the 'babyish' image when used by an individual learner.

✔ Money is an effective manipulative and is one step on to abstraction from a directly proportional manipulative such as base ten blocks. Also it is likely to be more acceptable for older learners.

Concrete materials and manipulatives

As a teacher who started his career as a teacher of chemistry and physics one of the strange anomalies of teaching mathematics for me is that, unlike science, the further the learner goes up the mathematics syllabus the less likely he is to use practical materials. Somewhere around about eight years old learners start to consider materials as patronising and babyish. Maybe this has something to do with the fact that some of these materials are bricks.

This can be circumvented by the teacher using the materials to demonstrate rather than the learner engaging in discovery 'play' with the material (those teaching philosophies from the 1960s die hard).

I think that one of the most important decisions a teacher makes is the choice of material(s) to illustrate a concept. It is likely, yet again, that the choice will be dependent on the learner. At least, in individual work, the focus should be the learner choosing a material that works for him rather than the teacher choosing *his* favourite material.

Materials have their own inherent characteristics. For example, a metre rule will give a linear image of units, tens, hundreds and thousands, whereas Dienes (base ten) blocks will give one, two and three dimensional images of units, tens, hundreds and thousands. Money is not proportional in size to the values it represents, but it is familiar and comes in easy number values based on 1, 2 and 5.

It seems to be stating the obvious, but the material must make the concept accessible. It must give the learner an unequivocal image of the idea that the symbols represent. The material and the symbols must be related in the learner's mind (rather than just the teacher's mind!)

Books and worksheets

✔ Work sheets and text book layouts can be overwhelming. They may use, for example, lots of small print, closely spaced or fussy, confused pages with cartoons and disjointed text. Try providing a cover sheet/window which reduces the quantity of material facing the pupil.

✔ The reading level may be beyond the pupil. If a book cannot be replaced in these economically hard times either provide a photocopied 'translation' or make sure you or a pupil reads the problem to the pupil with difficulties. This is particularly relevant for coursework and investigations.

✔ If a dyslexic pupil is having difficulty setting out work on the page discuss giving him an exercise book which has bigger/smaller/squares.

Homework

✔ Deal with the pupils who are forgetful and badly organised. Take a positive attitude and make sure they have the information and equipment they need. Parents of such pupils have usually suffered alongside their child as he struggles through school. You could try to liaise with them, for example by giving them a homework timetable. Remember, difficulties may be familial.

✔ Give homework in a form that they can access. For example check the vocabulary. Make sure the homework is read to the pupil before he takes it home. Get high tech and provide a disc so that work can be done on computer and could even have the facility of the PC reading the questions to the pupil.

✔ Consider allowing the pupil to use a calculator (with all the cautions I know you have about their use) or a number square or a table square.

Marking

✔ Mark new work before too many examples have been attempted. Do not let error patterns become ingrained.

✔ Mark diagnostically. For example, the pupil may have used the correct procedure, but made an arithmetical error. Do not just mark work 'wrong'. Say how it was wrong and what can be done to put it right.

✔ Remember the pupil who may work more slowly than his peers. Consider selecting fewer examples but still giving the breadth of experience.

✔ Be encouraging.

✔ Avoid red pens and big crosses and scribbles. (Try green and small and neat and, better still, constructive comments such as 'Small addition error here, rest OK.')

Remember

Pupils are individuals. Some will need some of these suggestions, some will survive without any of these suggestions. I do not think, however, that any learner will be disadvantaged by any of these suggestions and many will be advantaged. The suggestions may reduce some of the learning (special) needs in your classroom and even prevent the onset of some problems.

This book acknowledges that pupils are individuals. I have long had a suspicion of any scheme, intervention or cure that claims it is 'for all'. I suspect that the only part of this book that is 'for all' is the emphasis on understanding each pupil.

The Catch 22 of Catch Up

If a pupil falls behind he or she will have been working more slowly than their peers. To catch up he or she will have to progress faster than their peers. It is possible.

A few golden rules

- Don't create anxiety.
- Experiencing success reduces anxiety.
- Experiencing failure increases anxiety.
- Understand your pupils as individuals.
- Teach to the individual in the group . . . also known as the 'Teach more than one way to do things' rule.
- Remember where each topic leads mathematically.
- Understanding is a more robust outcome than just recall.
- Try to understand errors . . . don't just settle for 'wrong'.
- Prevention is better than cure.
- All the above rules have exceptions.

References

Ashcraft, M., Kirk, E.P. and Hopkins, D. (1998) 'On the cognitive consequences of mathematics anxiety', in Donlan, C. (ed.) *The Development of Mathematical Skills*. Hove, The Psychological Corporation.

Bakwin, H. and Bakwin, R.M. (1960) *Clinical Management of Behaviour Disorders in Children*. Philadelphia, Saunders.

Butterworth, B. (2003) *The Dyscalculia Screener*. London, NFER-Nelson.

Chinn, S.J. (1995) 'A pilot study to compare aspects of arithmetic skill', *Dyslexia Review* 4, pp. 4–7.

Chinn, S.J. and Ashcroft, J.R. (1992) 'The Use of Patterns' in T.R. Miles, and E. Miles, (eds) *Dyslexia and Mathematics*, London, Routledge.

Chinn, S.J. and Ashcroft, J.R. (1998) *Mathematics for Dyslexics: A Teaching Handbook*. London, Whurr.

Chinn, S.J., McDonagh, D., Van Elswijk, R., Harmsen, H., Kay, J., McPhillips, T., Power, A. and Skidmore, L. (2001) 'Classroom studies into cognitive style in mathematics for pupils with dyslexia in special education in the Netherlands, Ireland and the UK', *British Journal of Special Education*, 28, 2, pp. 80–5.

Cohn, R. (1968) 'Developmental dyscalculia', Pediatric Clinics of North America, 15, (3), pp. 651–68.

DfES (2001) *The National Numeracy Strategy: Guidance to Support Pupils with Dyslexia and Dyscalculia*. London, DfES.

Gerstmann, J. (1957) 'Some notes on the Gerstmann syndrome', *Neurology* 7, pp. 866–9.

Joffe, L. (1980) 'Dyslexia and attainment in school mathematics: Part 1', *Dyslexia Review*, 3 1, pp. 10–14.

Kosc, L. (1974) 'Developmental dyscalculia', *Journal of Learning Disabilities*, 7, 3, pp. 46–59.

Kosc, L. (1986) Dyscalculia. *Focus on Learning Problems in Mathematics*, 8, 3, 4.

Krutetskii, V.A. (1976) in Kilpatric, J. and Wirszup, I. (eds) *The Psychology of Mathematical Abilities in Schoolchildren*. Chicago, University of Chicago Press.

Magne, O. (1996) *Bibliography of Literature Dysmathematics Didakometry*. Malmo, Sweden.

Seligman, M. (1998) *Learned Optimism*. New York, Pocket Books.

Sharma, M.C. (1986) 'Dyscalculia and other learning problems in arithmetic: a historical perspective', *Focus on Learning Problems in Mathematics* 8, 3, 4, pp. 7–45.

Sharma, M. (1990) 'Dyslexia, dyscalculia and some remedial perspectives for mathematics learning problems.' *Math Notebook*, 8, 7–10.

Stanovich, K.E. (1991) 'The theoretical and practical consequences of discrepancy definitions of dyslexia.' In Snowling, M. and Thomsom M. (eds), *Dyslexia: Integrating Theory and Practise*. London, Whurr.

Chapter 2

Factors that affect learning

This chapter is about some of the factors which may contribute to a learner having difficulties with mathematics. Factors such as a poor short term memory can have a considerable impact on many of the topics that make up mathematics.

At the end of the section on each factor I have left space for the reader to add his or her own suggestions. I could never claim to know all the solutions, especially as it is so important to remember that what works for one student may well not work for another. Hence the need for a range of solutions, to be used in response to the individual needs of each learner.

Quite often the 'Suggestions' section includes the advice to 'take time and evaluate'. The culture of doing maths quickly can be totally opposite to the correct approach of appraising before reacting.

Some suggestions are immediate whilst others are long term.

Schools and colleges should work towards building up a bank/library of appropriate resources, so that many of these problems can be addressed from materials that have been prepared before.

Short term memory

The problem	Suggestions
Some children will have weaker short term memories than their peers. This may be a developmental lag or a persistent problem. What is relevant here, however, is the realisation that there will be a range of short term memory capacities among the pupils in any classroom.	
This will impact on the pupil's ability just to keep up with the lesson in general.	Do not give lengthy strings of instructions. Imagine someone giving you a ten digit phone number to

The problem (cont.)

Suggestions (cont.)

remember by presenting it, once, spoken quickly and with no breakdown into chunks of numbers. So present 712563449 as 712 563 449 or 71 25 63 44 9 or whatever chunking size pupils prefer.

In mental arithmetic it may be a challenge for them to remember the question.

Repeat the question, or put the key numbers on the board.

The procedure they are trying to use to solve the question may have too many steps for their short term memory capacity.

Ask what method they are trying to use. If appropriate suggest an alternative method, or accept an estimate. Perhaps allow them to make memory jottings for intermediate steps (halfway house to full mental work).

When attempting mental arithmetic questions they are handicapped by slow retrieval of basic facts.

Provide a table square or a basic addition facts square.
Give them questions which use the facts they do know (usually 2, 5, 10).

When copying questions from a page, worksheet or a board they only copy one or two or three items (letters or numbers) at a time and may mix up parts of questions, creating new extra questions.

Provide a worksheet which they can write on. Use colour or highlighters to help them to track their position on the board or worksheet. Mark the questions they create rather than the ones they should have done.

Remember, the easy option is for the learners to opt out and not try the work.

Be aware of this attitude, which will build into a major self esteem and attributional style issue.

Add your own suggestions and solutions (and extra problems!)

Mathematics memory

(This is long term memory for mathematical information).

The problem	Suggestions
Some pupils find instant recall from memory of basic addition facts a persistent problem, particularly in exams.	Allow finger counting (but be aware that this will not develop number skills). Teach pupils how to build on key addition facts such as doubles or number bonds for 10. For more detail see below. Teach pupils to write the number bonds for ten as their key facts and teach how to derive other facts from these bonds. Teach pupils how to draw up an addition square.
Some pupils find that instant recall of multiplication facts is a persistent problem.	Give pupils a multiplication square (and show them how to use it . . . for division too). Teach pupils how to create a multiplication square. Teach pupils strategies which build on the 'easy' facts. For example, double the 2× facts to obtain the 4× facts, or work out the 9× facts by working back from the 10× facts. For more detail see below.
A pupil cannot remember the long multiplication algorithm.	Teach repeated addition (in chunks of 2×, 5×, 10×, 20×, etc.). See Chapter 5.
A pupil cannot remember the division procedure.	Teach repeated subtraction (in chunks of 2×, 5×, 10×, 20×, etc.) See Chapter 5.

Add your own suggestions and solutions (and extra problems!)

Direction

The problem	Suggestions
Some children find the directionality of maths a challenge. The problem will be greatly exacerbated by inconsistencies such as division (see below).	
For example, some will find counting backwards problematic, more so than you, the teacher might predict.	This will require more practise, perhaps asking for smaller sequences of reverse order numbers, starting with 'one less, one back from x'. Start from different numbers. Try counting back in 2s, 5s, 10s (also as 76, 66, 56, 46 . . . as well as 70, 60, 50, 40 . . .). Then introduce 9s and relate to 10s. Try counting to a target number 18, 16, 14, _, _, _, 6, 4. Point out patterns, using colour to highlight the pattern.
The pupil hears 'Nineteen' and writes 91 (which actually follows the order of the word, as is the case for all the 'teen' numbers).	The teen numbers are the exceptional two digit numbers, with the unit digit coming before the ten (teen). See Transposals, p. 36.
They may also find the change from positive coordinates to negative coordinates disproportionately more difficult.	A chance to remind learners to look for detail, to absorb before reacting. Perhaps the learner could label the axes negative and positive boldly and appropriately. Refer back to work on the number line. This may pre-empt the problem.
Children may also be phased by the change in direction of the steps for traditional short and long division compared to the right to left working for addition, subtraction and multiplication.	Teach alternate methods, for example repeated addition or subtraction.
Confusion may arise over the different ways in which division is represented, for example 54 divided by 9 can be written as:	Make sure you do not assume pupils will automatically take on board these representations. Explain the meaning alongside the alternatives.

The problem (cont.)	*Suggestions (cont.)*
$54 \div 9$ or $9\overline{)54}$ or $\frac{54}{9}$	In the $\div$ symbol the dots are replaced with the numbers of the fraction, that is, in this example the dots are replaced by 54 (on the top) and 9.
The sequence of place values as you move left or right of the decimal point may confuse, especially when the language is considered as in hundreds and hundredths.	Show the digits as you say the words. Use a visual image or concrete material such as base ten blocks. 'This is one ten*th*, one divided into ten equal parts, $\frac{1}{10}$' or money with 10p as $\frac{1}{10}$ of £1. The relationship between $\frac{1}{10}$ and 10 can be considered with 10p and £10, bringing in language and rewording such as 'How many 10p's in £10?' compared to the abstract '10 divided by $\frac{1}{10}$' (which also rephrases a division question as a multiplication question).

Add your own suggestions and solutions (and extra problems!)

Visual

The problem	*Suggestions*
Think about the 'look' of a page, a worksheet, a test.	Look carefully at presentation when choosing text books or when designing a worksheet. (See also Speed of Working, p.27.)
If the presentation is crowded, with little space between lines or questions, then some pupils will experience anxiety.	Illustrations may help the look of a page. They should be pertinent. If lines of print are set too close then pupils may mix up lines, taking some information from one line and the next inappropriately from another line. Try providing the pupil with a piece of card with a window or slot cut into it so only a part of the page is revealed.
In an attempt to be more user-friendly some book designers have made the layout very fragmented.	Look for simple, clear design. Try the window strategy (above).
The symbols for the four operations can be confusing if not written or	Choose a clear font at a suitable size. Also be wary of learners

The problem (cont.)

printed carefully.
A + can be close to a ÷. A little
rotation can make a + and a ×
indistinguishable

Pupils may mix up questions, taking
part from one line and part from the
line below.

The page seems blurred.

The pupil finds copying from the
board a problem.

Pupils cannot draw a 2D
representation of a 3D figure, for
example a cuboid.

Suggestions (cont.)

perseverating, that is continuing to
add, for example when the problems
have changed to subtract. The pressure
of working quickly can exacerbate this
problem, as can anxiety. Encourage
the learner to relax and to sub-vocalise
the symbols or highlight them.

Line off questions or space them out.
Try a coloured overlay. Black print on
white paper blurs the images for some
readers. (Suppliers I.O.O. Marketing,
City University, London: admin@ioo
marketing.co.uk).
Mark the question they have created
rather than the one in the book!

Try a coloured overlay. Try printing
worksheets on coloured paper.
Try different coloured print.
Suggest a visit to a specialist
optometrist.

Provide a handout or use coloured
pens to break up information.
Keep presentation clear and well
spaced out. Try not to talk when
pupils are copying. (Some pupils
cannot dual task, i.e. listen and write
at the same time.)

Try providing isometric paper.
Show how the drawing of a cuboid is
made up of two off-set rectangles
joined by parallel lines.

Add your own suggestions and solutions (and extra problems!)

Speed of working

The problem	*Suggestions*
Teachers often expect learners to do mental arithmetic problems quickly.	Allow selected pupils to have a little more time. For example, ask the question, say you will come back to them, ask another learner (or two) and then return for the answer. Slow recall of basic facts may be the slowing influence. Give the pupil a table square or an addition square. Give part of the answer, for example, asking for 64 + 78, ask for the unit digit: '64 plus 78 is one hundred and forty . . .' or structure 'What is 8 add 4? What is 60 add 70 add 10?'
Pupils may find homework (and class) tasks difficult to finish.	Set fewer questions, but ensure the pupil gets to experience the range, as in setting, say, the even number questions (thus revising that concept too). Provide worksheets where the pupils fill in gaps rather than writing out all of the question. Don't overface the learner.
Pupils take an impulsive approach to the maths problems.	For word problems, encourage them to read through a problem, rephrase it, draw it if possible. For number problems encourage them to verbalise it, for example for 85 − 17, sub-vocalise, '85 minus 17; 85 take away 17' using different phrasing.
Pupils are slow to even start work. There could be several reasons . . . They did not hear all the instructions (poor short term memory, inattention, distractions, hearing).	Repeat instructions, chunking them, not giving too many steps at once. Make sure he has heard by asking him (quietly and individually, to repeat the instructions).
They are avoiding the work (anxiety, attribution, attitude).	The first two reasons need long term nurture (see Chapter 8). Attitude could be due to several causes and needs, initially, empathetic discussion.

The problem (cont.)	Suggestions (cont.)
Pupils fail to finish a test within the set time.	Provide them with a different coloured pen or pencil and allow them to carry on until they have tried as many of the items as they feel they can attempt.
They haven't got all the necessary equipment (book, pen, calculator).	If there is a support assistant, this could be part of their brief. Establish a routine. For example have equipment ready to give out and have a system to make sure it is returned (mark it clearly!). (More suggestions in 'No attempts'.)

Add your own suggestions and solutions (and extra problems!)

No attempts

The problem	Suggestions
A pupil leaves lots of unanswered questions.	Pupils who think they can't succeed at a question may decide to not try rather than get it wrong, this is in part an anxiety/attitude problem. So check if they understand the topic and ask what it is that is making them not attempt the work. 'What is it you don't understand?' (Do not accept, 'Maths' as an answer! Ask them to be specific, this is a diagnostic question.) Is there a pattern to the missed questions? (More diagnosis.) Were they absent when that topic was taught?
A pupil is slow to start work.	It could be that the pupil is badly organised . . . can't find book, pen, etc. If this is a regular occurrence, have a 'buddy' pupil pack for him. You may even get it back at the end of the lesson!
	It could be that avoidance of failure. Try asking him to attempt just one or two questions. (This has another very important benefit. If a pupil makes an error in his first practise of a new topic, that error pattern will establish

The problem (cont.)	*Suggestions (cont.)*
	itself, setting up the need for intensive remediation in the future.)
	Try sitting the pupil at the back of the class so you can walk over to him and focus him without the other pupils noticing him. This could be negotiated instead of sitting him at the front where everyone sees the reminders.
A pupil has no idea how to begin.	Offer a starting hint or do the first line. Offer a model answer.
A pupil starts the exercise, but gives up after two or three questions.	This could be the 'quantum leap' effect. Some exercises and worksheets start with two or three relatively straightforward and easy questions and then, 'Wham' the next question is so very much harder that the pupil goes into the 'No attempt' strategy. Check the worksheet or exercise by actually doing the questions and imagining you are that pupil. Then modify the work.

Add your own suggestions and solutions (and extra problems!)

Recording/writing up

The problem	*Suggestions*
The pupil only writes an answer. There is no record of the method/ procedure used.	This may be a consequence of a 'grasshopper' thinking style (Chapter 4). Pupils should be encouraged to discuss their methods and be shown how to record their methods. This could be done by the teacher modelling the technique or providing an exemplar answer 'frame'.
The pupil writes very cursory notes.	This may be a consequence of slow writing skills rather than the pupil not knowing what to do. Allow more time and/or reduce the number of examples he is required to do. Provide a sheet with the key vocabulary.

The problem (cont.)

Writing is extremely untidy and disorganised.

Suggestions (cont.)

Try squared paper of variously sized squares until a suitable one is found. Offer a worksheet where the writing demands are minimised. Allow the pupil opportunities to talk through his methods so he can show his abilities.

Copying from the board. This requires the student to look up, focus on the board, find the correct place, remember some data, refocus on his paper/book, write the data in the correct space, refocus on the board and repeat the procedure. This is very influenced by short term memory.

Offer notes. Allow him to photocopy the notes from a student who produces good notes.
If the material is in a text book, allow him to highlight key areas.
Check, regularly that he has adequate (or better) notes.
Provide notes.

Add your own suggestions and solutions (and extra problems!)

Poor recall of basic facts

The problem

The pupil makes many basic fact errors, such as $7 + 6 = 12$ or $6 \times 7 = 67$ within 'longer' computations.

Suggestions

Have a supply of basic fact squares (expect losses).
Supply a calculator, suggesting it is just used to access the basic facts rather than doing the whole calculation.
Show how to make a number bonds for ten chart

$$10\ 9\ 8\ 7\ 6\ 5\ 4\ 3\ 2\ 1\ 0$$

$$0\ \ 1\ 2\ 3\ 4\ 5\ 6\ 7\ 8\ 9\ 10$$

(note the emphasis for 5, acting as a check) and show how to use it to obtain other facts.

Poor knowledge of basic factors handicaps factorising quadratic equations.

Teach some patterns to reduce the extent of the problem, such as looking for even numbers (2 and 4), 5s and 0s, digits adding to 9, digits adding to 3, 6 or 9 (3).
Provide a table square and revise how to use it for factors (division).

The problem (cont.)	*Suggestions (cont.)*
	Show how to fill in a blank table square and see above. Make sure the early questions involve only simple factors, so the pupil can focus on learning the procedure.

Add your own suggestions and solutions (and extra problems!)

Poor reading skills

The problem	*Suggestions*
The pupil has difficulty in reading.	Check if he needs spectacles or a better (and possibly bigger) print (many photocopiers can enlarge print). Try a coloured overlay to change the print/paper contrast (suppliers I.O.O. Marketing, see Appendix 2).
The pupil has difficulty in reading word problems (but understands them if they are read to him).	Read them to him. (Though this takes your time and may damage his self-esteem if not done discretely and with empathy.) Provide him with a personal dictionary, with the necessary vocabulary for this topic – previously read, explained and discussed. Check the non-mathematical vocabulary (names, places, etc.). Change it to easily decodable alternatives, for example, Ocraville to Bath). Scan the work into a computer and let the pupil use voice output.
The pupil has difficulty in understanding/interpreting word problems.	Encourage the pupil to reword the question. Encourage the pupil to try and represent the problem as pictures. Try one of the reading acronyms, e.g. SQ3R . . . Survey, Question, Read, Review, Respond. (If nothing else it counteracts impulsivity.) Give number sentences and encourage learners to create word problems for themselves (see Chapter 6).

Add your own suggestions and solutions (and extra problems!)

Sequencing skills

The problem	*Suggestions*
Pupils have difficulty remembering and recalling sequential information.	Point out and demonstrate the pattern. Don't wait too long for the learner to discover the sequence for himself.
Number sequence for 2 beyond 10.	Start with the part they can recall 2, 4, 6, 8 (who do we appreciate) and use it as a base, pointing out the patterns 12, 14, 16, 18 . . . 22, 24, 26, 28 . . . possibly using coins or base ten blocks. This can also be a task where the learner progresses from counting on. The difference between numbers is two each time.
Number sequences for 10 when the unit digit is not zero. The pupil can recall 10, 20, 30, 40 . . . but finds sequences such as 13, 23, 33 . . . challenging.	A good chance to enhance place value concepts. Again use coins or base ten blocks to show the pattern. This time the units digit is the stable factor. The difference between consecutive numbers is ten each time. Use a 1 to 100 number square and point out/colour in the 'plus 10' patterns.
General number sequences.	Encourage the pupil to work out the differences between consecutive numbers and thus know if the difference is always the same or if the differences create a new sequence (finding the 'bridge' between numbers). For sequences such as adding (or subtracting) 6, 7, 8 or 9 each time suggest that the addition or subtraction be done using the easy numbers. So, to add 6, add as 5 and 1 or to subtract 9 take away 10 and add back 1.
Incorrect decimal sequence as . . . 0.7, 0.8, 0.9, *0.10*	Use 10p coins alongside the written numbers; that is, write the decimal and place the coins, write the next decimal and add another coin. Discuss where the 0.1, 0.2, . . . sequence is heading. It is heading for 1.0.

The problem (cont.)

Suggestions (cont.)

Offer a sequence with gaps . . . 0.1, 0.2, __, 0.4, __, __, 0.7, 0.8, __, __, 1.1, __, 1.3.

Incorrect fraction sequence as . . .$\frac{1}{10}$, $\frac{1}{11}$, $\frac{1}{12}$ where the learner assumes that $\frac{1}{12}$ is the biggest of the three fractions.

Go back to the fractions that (should) be known, i.e., half, quarter and third and place these in order of size. Demonstrate with folded paper. Discuss sharing slices of cake and pizza, but remember that these are not true fractions. Use a clock (time) for halves and quarters. Establish the concept that fractions involve division. Remind them that fractions cannot be taken at face value. Learners have to look beyond the numbers that they see or write.

Procedural sequences/algorithms (e.g. long division).

Try to support memory with understanding.
Find an alternative procedure that relates to the pupil's thinking style (see Chapter 4).
Find a mnemonic (e.g. BODMAS) but do not use this strategy too often lest the mnemonics themselves become another burden on memory.

Pupils have difficulty entering data into a calculator in the correct sequence as in 'Take 16 from 47' or 7)542.

Encourage the pupil to be wary, not rush and write the problem in symbols then appraise and compare the original question and its symbolic form.

Pupils have difficulty continuing a sequence if it does not start at the beginning as in 'What is the next number after 6?' The learner goes back to 1, 2, 3, 4, 5, 6 . . . 7.

Show the whole sequence, for example with wood or plastic numbers, then take away some of the beginning numbers and/or some of the end numbers.
Show how to identify the interval (gap) between consecutive numbers in the sequence.
Say a series of numbers and ask the pupil to join in at different points.
Show parts of sequences, for example, 46, 48, 50, 52 . . . or 34, 39, 44, 49, 54 . . . and ask pupils to identify the sequence.

Add your own suggestions and solutions (and extra problems!)

Transfer of skills

The problem	Suggestions
The pupil can only add when the numbers are presented in the standard vertical format.	Practise the skill in a 'problem' context, working from the digits to simple language, 'Add 46 and 88' to more complex language . . . in small steps.
The pupil can combine 2×8 with 5×8, but cannot combine $2x + 5x$.	Demonstrate the transition with, say, number rods.

Add your own suggestions and solutions (and extra problems!)

The 'terminal' inchworm/grasshopper (see Chapter 4)

The problem	Suggestions
The pupil will only respond to and work in one thinking mode. His thinking style is fixed at one end of the continuum.	If, after much empathetic intervention the learner's thinking style remains inflexible, then you, the teacher will have to work with that situation. This will mean accepting the learner as he is and giving him the skills to succeed using only a restricted thinking style. One consequence may well be that he has to learn how to identify questions that are unchangeably grasshopper and not waste time trying to answer them. This is pragmatism at a level that will sit uncomfortably with many teachers, but it may be the kindest (and most effective) way of teaching these rareish pupils.

Add your own suggestions and solutions (and extra problems!)

Order

The problem	Suggestions
The learner hears 'Ten past seven' and writes 10:7.	Time is one of those topics which is so familiar in everyday use that we may forget the problems it generates. The learner should be taught to repeat the time putting in hours and minutes, 'Ten minutes past seven hours' and know that the written convention is 'Hours: minutes'.
The learner reads 'Take 8 away from 18' and writes 8 − 18.	The learner must be taught to be wary of even the most innocent looking word problems and rephrase them until they make sense. The fact that 8 − 18 either looks impossible or leads to a negative answer should suggest caution.
In an addition sum such as 56 + 37, the learner adds 6 and 7 to make 13, writes down 1 and carries 3.	The teen numbers are misleading in that the unit syllable comes before the tens syllable. See Chapter 6.

Add your own suggestions and solutions (and extra problems!)

Not checking an answer

The problem	Suggestions
The learner checks (often quickly and inadequately).	Try to encourage checking by an alternative method. This links to encouraging flexible thinking styles (see Chapter 4). Try to encourage a check via an estimate. Ask 'Does the answer make sense?' Use the basic estimate question, 'Is the answer bigger or smaller?' (adjusted to make contextual sense).
The learner doesn't check at all.	Ask him what rough value (for numeracy) he expected the answer would be. Allow a wide guess/estimate and edge him towards closer estimates. This could be part of the training towards risk taking.

Add your own suggestions and solutions (and extra problems!)

Organisation

The problem	Suggestions
The pupil always arrives at lessons without key equipment.	Suggest he obtains a pencil case or similar holder in which to keep just the essentials. Be prepared to lend equipment, but be even more prepared to remember to collect it back at the end of the lesson. (He will forget.) Make sure the equipment you lend is clearly marked!
The pupil's written work on the page is badly organised.	Try squared paper, offering different sizes of square to find what suits. Try vertical lines. Try modelling good layout. Try a worksheet where part of the work is written (differentiation).

Add your own suggestions and solutions (and extra problems!)

Transposals

The problem	Suggestions
The pupil transposes numbers, for example he writes 31 for thirteen. This is likely to be the consequence of the words we use for the 'teen' numbers. These are the only two digit numbers where the units digit is named first as in *four*teen.	Try place value cards (Figure 2.1) or coins to model the correct digit order. (Check if transposals only occur for teen numbers, where the words do mislead, as in thirteen . . . three ten, rather than twenty-three which does not.) Explain the language structure of a teen number compared to the digit structure.

Explain that the teen numbers are exceptional and to be wary when they are around. Show how transposals can be a problem when adding numbers as 27 + 36 becoming 81 instead of 63 since 7 + 6 is added as 31. Encourage the learner to evaluate such answers by estimates.

Play card search games, with cards that show, for example, 16 and 61 and ask for 'sixteen' or 'sixty-one'.

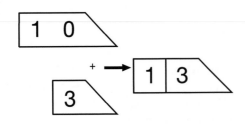

Figure 2.1 Place value cards

Add your own suggestions and solutions (and extra problems!)

Generalisations and recognising patterns

The problem	*Suggestions*
The learner does not recognise patterns.	
Some lessons rely on pupils making the discovery of a pattern. This may not always be a reliable method (for example, a pupil may process in groups of three and the pattern may be in groups of four).	Be more overt in hinting at the pattern. Use colours. Use materials (use trial and error to find the match between learner and material). For example base ten blocks may work as an illustration of multiplying and dividing by 10, possibly in conjunction with a place value sheet.

Add your own suggestions and solutions (and extra problems!)

Task analysis

In order to be pre-emptive, it may be worth doing a task analysis for a new topic. This can be a quick procedure, just thinking about the topic and making notes on the sheet below. The analysis can consider the topic, of course, but it can also take into consideration the nature of the learner(s). For example if the group contains a number of students with language problems then you might give more thought to that particular aspect of the task. A task analysis can be useful in focusing attention on areas where some pre-emptive action may greatly reduce the number of learners developing a problem with the topic and/or reduce the intensity of the problems (Figures 2.2 and 2.3, shown overleaf).

Analysing from the pre-requisite sub-skills perspective (Chapter 4) may also help a tutor/teacher understand where learning may falter.

TOPIC		
Factor	Problem	Suggestion
Vocabulary and symbols		
Language		
Short term memory		
Long term memory		
Sequences		
Direction		
Organisation/ spatial		
Thinking style		

Figure 2.2 A blank task analysis form

TOPIC	Mental addition of two digit plus two digit numbers	
Factor	Problem	Suggestion
Vocabulary and symbols	A variety of words imply +	Vary the vocabulary of the questions: 'What is 46 *add* 72?' '43 *plus* 56?' 'What is the *total* of 61 and 39?'
Language	Should not be an issue with mental addition, unless wrapped up in a complicated story.	
Short term memory	May not remember the question. May not have enough short term memory to do the question.	Repeat the question. Try an alternate method. Ask a part question.
Long term memory	The usual problem of recall of basic facts, and possibly of 'carrying'.	Use sums with known facts, e.g. 74 + 75, so doubles can be used.
Sequences	Not a main problem in this topic, but the answer may be computed in the reverse order, e.g. 74 + 75 done as 9 then 14.	Encourage pre-estimates and allow time for this or ask in two stages, that is first ask for an estimate and then the accurate answer.
Direction	Since 64 + 56 = 56 + 64 this should not be a problem, but see 'sequences'.	
Organisation/ spatial	Should not be a factor in mental work, but spatial memory may be needed.	
Thinking style	The pupil may use a method that is less suitable for his learning problems.	Encourage alternative strategies. Ask the pupil to evaluate and inter-relate the numbers, e.g. 8 and 9 can be rounded up to 10.

Figure 2.3 An example of a task analysis

Chapter 3

What the curriculum asks pupils to do and where difficulties may occur

In the last chapter I looked at factors, for example, poor short term memory, which could create learning difficulties for mathematics. In this chapter I am looking at topics in mathematics and how they could create difficulties in learning.

This chapter is based on the English National Numeracy Strategy, but it is likely to be similar to the development of different strands and topics in many numeracy schemes across the world. What I have done is to take the Year 5 (age 9 years) teaching programme as typical of the content of the NNS Framework, highlighted the key issues, predicted where difficulties and confusions might arise and outlined some possible solutions. Some of these are dealt with in more detail in other chapters, but to avoid the need to flick between pages, I have kept the content somewhat self contained. The chapter illustrates analysis of content in terms of its likely interactions with learners. A similar analysis could be applied to any programme of work. This is the preventative medicine. Whatever the curriculum, the analogy I like is to compare preparing a mathematics lesson to preparing an expedition. You prepare for all the many problems you know you are going to encounter, and experience helps you to predict what they will be, but then experience tells you that there will still be some problems you will not have predicted. The curriculum is the guide to the journey. This chapter is the guide to some of the unpredicted events that may prevent your learners from having a successful expedition.

The programme for Year 5 of the National Numeracy Strategy: numbers and the number system

Place value, ordering and rounding

This section deals with basic, fundamentally important topics which set the foundations for success in numeracy. Much of this section and, indeed the complete 'Numbers and the Number System' is inter-linked and each part should support understanding of the other parts. You should not assume that pupils absorb these links by osmosis. Many will need explicit teaching. It is easy to assume that an ability for recall means understanding.

Most of this work is within the pupils' experiences. This is both a positive and negative factor. It is positive in the sense that pupils are working from familiar facts and awareness, but negative in that they may already have formed some incorrect ideas or feel that because the work is familiar they do not need to organise, strengthen and inter-relate their fact base to new work.

Place value is a key concept. Children who fail to grasp the idea of place value find numeracy difficult and make errors such as:

$$\begin{array}{r} 45 \\ +88 \\ \hline 12\ 13 \end{array} \qquad \begin{array}{r} 45 \\ +88 \\ \hline 123 \end{array}$$

Misconceptions can arise from early experiences. For example, we start number as 1, 2, 3, 4, 5 . . . where the sequence 'gets bigger' as we track to the right. When place value arises, as with, say 24, the number to the left is 'bigger'.

Subtraction, especially involving decomposition will also be handicapped by poor understanding of place value. Equally multiplication by the traditional methods requires that place values are understood, so that, for example when multiplying by 45 the pupil needs to know and understand that the 4 is 40 and what effect this has on the multiplication. Pupils need to be able to break down numbers. This includes using place value as well as number relationships, for example 25 as $100 \div 4$ or 99 as $100 - 1$.

Manipulatives can be helpful, particularly base ten blocks and coins to give a visual image to the symbolic representations of numbers. Numbers which involve zero (such as 5004) often need extra explanation and again base ten materials may help. Try working from 5444, through 5044 to 5004 using the base ten blocks. Multiplying and dividing by 10 and powers of 10 may also help to show how the position of a number affects its value.

All the work on placing a number in the correct position on a number line and the linked work on estimation leads pupils to overview skills. Estimation is a holistic skill and should be taught to complement the procedural skills of written arithmetic, even though pupils may show a marked preference towards one of these skills. Remember that estimation is not precise and that the required level of 'accuracy' of the estimation depends on the particular real life situation. The 'empty' number line is a good visual for practising this skill.

Rounding strengthens estimation in the sense of 'levels' by rounding to the nearest ten, nearest hundred, nearest thousand. It is also a good real life skill, particularly useful for shopping.

The introduction to negative numbers uses everyday examples. Later pupils may come to forget the reality at the root of negative numbers and see them as a very abstract concept. This introductory work on adding to a negative number ($-3°C$ and warming up by $4°C$) and subtracting from a negative number ($-3°C$ and cooling down by a further $4°C$) sets the foundation to work from an image that is 'real' to an abstract and symbolic representation ($-3 + 4 = 1$ and $-3 - 4 = -7$). This topic also introduces the idea that addition and subtraction are opposite versions of the same idea.

The quite sophisticated sequence 10, 9, 8, 7, 6, 5, 4, 3, 2, 1, 0, −1, −2, −3, −4 . . . takes a familiar reverse counting skill beyond the zero and the rules of number sequence are now reversed. In positive numbers 4 is bigger than 3. In negative numbers −4 is smaller than −3. In early number work these 'abnormalities' can confuse tentative learning and need that explicit teaching.

Properties of numbers and number sequences

This section of the programme could be treated as largely rote learning. However, there will be some pupils who fail to rote learn facts. There will be other pupils who merely learn and do not understand. It will be important to identify both groups of these pupils and help them circumvent these early barriers which could result in an anxiety about maths which could then lead them to not being involved in future learning. The section could be used as a good opportunity to develop confidence with numbers by showing how frequently patterns occur and how frequently these same patterns can help with remembering and accessing facts and working with numbers. The inter-relationship between numbers, especially relating numbers to the 'reference' numbers of 2, 5 and 10 will build better recall and understanding for ALL pupils. The goal is to making the acquisition of skills and understanding robust.

Using strategies to access facts is an early indicator of a 'grasshopper' learning style, that is an intuitive way with numbers and an ability to break down and build up numbers into more convenient values, e.g. using 100 instead of 98. (See Chapter 4.)

Recognise and extend number sequences

This area sets many basic procedures and understandings in place and, although perhaps deceptively simple or ordinary, needs attention so that understanding and as much automaticity as possible is achieved.

Counting on in 6s, 7s, 8s, and 9s and 11s (to a lesser extent) will be problematic for some pupils. The patterns and relationships ($6 = 5 + 1$, $7 = 5 + 2$, $8 = 10 - 2$, $9 = 10 - 1$ and $11 = 10 + 1$) will be essential strategies for some pupils and useful, reinforcing processes for others.

There are repeating patterns when counting on in 6s, 8s, 9s and 11s. These need to be clearly demonstrated to ensure all pupils absorb and then recreate the patterns. It will help to use visual support for any oral presentations. Number lines, Cuisinaire rods and coins, used alongside the numbers, would suit these topics.

Number rods are good to show the 9 sequence against a metre rule marked in decimetres, showing a one less comparison each time. This is good for 8 rods too, reinforced with the repeating pattern in the unit digits of 8, 6, 4, 2, 0, which is giving number connection support by using $10 - 2 = 8$ (on 10 back 2 for addition and back 10 on 2 for subtraction).

This also compares with adding and subtracting 9 and 11, where 9 is computed as $10 - 1$ and 11 is done as $10 + 1$. Also adding and subtracting 6 can be done as 5 and 1 and 7 as 5 and 2.

All these examples are relating 'harder' numbers to the base numbers of 5 and 10, building on what pupils know, rather than just adding in extra, unrelated information. You are giving memory an extra source of support.

Look out for the common error in the decimal sequence, 0.1 0.2 0.3 ... 0.8 0.9 0.10 ('nought point ten'). A supporting visual image such as coins, or a number line should help. It is important to pre-empt this error, so that it does not become that all too influential first experience of this important concept of the transition from a decimal number to a whole number.

Counting backwards is often much harder than counting forwards. Do not assume learners will exhibit equal facility with these two tasks.

Even and odd numbers

Even numbers end (have a units digit) in 0, 2, 4, 6 or 8. Every other digit can be odd, it's that last one that matters, e.g. 975,31**2** is even.

Odd numbers end (have a units digit) in 1, 3, 5, 7 or 9. Every other digit can be even, it's the last one that matters, e.g. 864,20**7** is odd.

Establish (or re-establish) the main idea that even numbers are about 2, about being exactly divisible by 2 (an early exposure to the concept of division). And an even number plus 1 makes an odd number.

Use any even Cuisenaire rod, say a 6 rod and place a 1 rod on the end. Show this is the same value as a 7 rod. Review the reasons why 6 is even and 7 is odd. Now show side by side two '6 rod plus 1 rod' and pair the 1 rods to show that the combination is even ... two odd numbers add to make an even number. Now show three '6 rod plus 1 rod' then four and five to develop the pattern of combining odd and even numbers. Repeat for other values. Demonstrate the same pattern for subtraction, referring to the similarities with addition.

Recognise multiples of 6, 7, 8 and 9

The alternative approaches are straight recall or strategies built on patterns. Rote learning will work for many, but the successful rote learners also will benefit from learning to recognise patterns and using them to support and develop their facility with numbers. There is good scope for visual images to reinforce oral patterns.

Show the patterns in each of these series, for example the 6, 2, 8, 4, 0 pattern in the units for $6\times$, the 'adding up to 9' pattern for $9\times$ facts ($6 \times 9 = 54$ ... $5 + 4 = 9$). Reinforce the multiples of 7 which are known from other times tables, for example 9×7, 2×7 (thus 4×7), 5×7 and 10×7.

Know and apply tests of divisibility by 2, 4, 5, 10 or 100

◆ This is another chance to reinforce the use of patterns and inter-relationships of numbers and to relate multiplication and division.
◆ Recognising an even number will identify divisibility by 2 and will lead to testing divisibility by 4 (dividing by 2 twice is an alternative).
◆ The 5 pattern is good for predicting if the answer will have a units digit of 5 or 0, that is be an odd or even number, thus providing further reinforcement of that concept.
◆ Introduce 'factor' using multiplication examples as well as division (for example, a pair of factors of 15 is 3 and 5, 15 is divisible by 3 and by 5, and $3 \times 5 = 15$) ... relating multiplication and division again.

Fractions, decimals and percentages, ratio and proportion

Inter-relating these ways of representing numbers less than one (and bigger than one of course) will reinforce the understanding of each format. Keep referring to the common equivalents using them to provide 'markers' and illustrate other examples:

$$\tfrac{1}{2} = 0.5 = 50\%, \ \tfrac{1}{4} = 0.25 = 25\%, \ \tfrac{1}{10} = 0.1 = 10\%, \ \tfrac{3}{4} = 0.75 = 75\%$$

Use fraction notation and vocabulary: change an improper fraction to a mixed number, etc.

Fractions are radically different in that they incorporate a (disguised) division sign and use two numbers. The introductory explanations set the foundations of the concept of fractions, relating them to everyday knowledge, building on an existing awareness that needs organisation and mathematical understanding. Using half and quarter can provide a secure base to refer back to as knowledge develops.

The vocabulary for fractions can be used to aid comprehension, e.g. $\tfrac{4}{5}$ can be translated as 4 divided by 5 or 4 out of 5 equal parts or four fifths. Each of these translations needs explicit explanation and clear visual images. The explanations must ensure that the visual images are accurately related to the symbols. For example, working from the familiar image of a clock face gives an image of half and quarter (remember that these two fractions are vocabulary exceptions, unlike one tenth or one twenty sixth). The familiar fractions $\tfrac{1}{2}$, $\tfrac{1}{4}$ and $\tfrac{3}{4}$ can be used to establish the vocabulary and idea of numerator and denominator. Although it is a reasonable expectation that pupils should and can manage these two words, for some pupils they will be a barrier to further understanding. Use alternative clear vocabulary alongside the accepted labels. The clock face can be used to explore all the interpretations built around fractions, e.g. the division into two equal parts, two halves are one whole (but beware the other meaning 'hole') the adding of $\tfrac{1}{4}$ to $\tfrac{1}{4}$ to make $\tfrac{2}{4}$ (don't let pupils leap to $\tfrac{1}{2}$ without understanding the idea involved, equivalent fractions, that is $\tfrac{1}{4} + \tfrac{1}{4} = \tfrac{2}{4} = \tfrac{1}{2}$. Also introduce $\tfrac{6}{12}$, $\tfrac{3}{12}$, $\tfrac{30}{60}$ and $\tfrac{15}{60}$). Extend to the adding of $\tfrac{1}{2}$ and $\tfrac{1}{4}$ to make $\tfrac{3}{4}$. The frequent misconception of big numbers making fractions of big values can be addressed by building on $\tfrac{1}{4}$ being smaller than $\tfrac{1}{2}$ and $\tfrac{1}{60}$ (1 minute) being smaller than $\tfrac{1}{2}$. Another important understanding can be based on fundamental fractions, the idea that $\tfrac{2}{2}$ and $\tfrac{4}{4}$ are 1 and then onto $\tfrac{3}{2}$ and $\tfrac{5}{4}$ and $1\tfrac{1}{2}$ and $1\tfrac{1}{4}$.

The concepts or the misunderstandings of fractions often begin when working with these first examples.

Other everyday images could be included such as 50p as half of one pound (100p) which will eventually lead to the connection with decimal fractions. Two 50p coins could be shown as equivalent to £1 and add to the concept of equivalent fractions.

Folding squares of paper can act as a good visual image. It also keeps the developmental model of area in mind. Folding one square shows fractions such as $\tfrac{1}{2}$, $\tfrac{1}{3}$, $\tfrac{1}{4}$, $\tfrac{1}{6}$ and some image of the inter-relationships. Folding two or more squares shows an early introduction to, say $3 \times \tfrac{1}{4}$. This can be done by folding three sheets of paper to $\tfrac{1}{4}$ to compare with looking at three quarters on one sheet. (See Chapter 10.)

Relate fractions to division

Operations such as '$\frac{1}{4}$ of 8' challenge some previous ideas and need more explanation than just learning a rule or procedure. A clear understanding of this type of question is another step towards secure work with fractions. Pupils will probably relate 'of' to multiply. Previous experience of 'multiply' is that the answer is bigger, which tallies with everyday language use of multiply. Set up the basic first question, 'Is the answer the same, bigger or smaller?' This could develop into a follow-up question, 'Is it a lot smaller ($\frac{1}{100}$ of £5) or just a bit smaller ($\frac{3}{4}$ of 8)?

Explain that $\frac{3}{4} \times 8$ decodes/translates to $3 \times 8 \div 4$ or $8 \div 4 \times 3$. This highlights the 'hidden' divide sign and shows that the times or divide can be done in either order.

Use decimal notation for tenths and hundredths

Pupils will be familiar with money written as £3.49. This can be used to give an image of $\frac{1}{10}$, 0.1 and $\frac{1}{100}$, 0.01. Base ten blocks can be used to provide a proportional model. If pupils are having difficulty, show each decimal with money and base ten blocks. Add on coins or blocks, 0.1 and 0.01 to make new numbers. Discuss the place value, as base ten, coins and symbols (digits).

There can be a language and order/direction confusion here for some pupils. Whole numbers progress from right to left as units, tens, hundreds, getting bigger, whilst decimals go right to left as tenths and hundredths, getting smaller and with only a slight change in the sound of the words.

Round a number with one or two decimal places to the nearest integer

The similarity of this process to whole number rounding should be explained. The use of shop prices such as £9.99 can be discussed.

Relate fractions to their decimal representation

Focus on the key values of $\frac{1}{2}$ and 0.5 (It may help some pupils to discuss 0.5 and 0.50. Another directional difference with whole numbers, 0.5 and 0.50 are the same value whereas 5 and 50 are not and 05 is used rarely – sometimes on forms for months, 05 being May, or in 24 hour timetables). and $\frac{1}{4}$ and 0.25, $\frac{1}{10}$ and 0.1, $\frac{1}{100}$ and 0.01. Set up a table and start to fill in some gaps, such as 0.2 which is $\frac{1}{5}$ (not $\frac{1}{20}$). Show how decimals can be combined, such as 0.3 and 0.5 to make 0.8 and compare this, without calculations, to combining fractions such as $\frac{3}{10}$ and $\frac{1}{2}$. Calculations for fractions to decimals can be shown with a calculator, especially if patterns are demonstrated ($\frac{100}{2} = 50$, $\frac{10}{2} = 5$, $\frac{1}{2} = 0.5$ and $\frac{100}{10} = 10$, $\frac{10}{10} = 1$ and $\frac{1}{10} = 0.1$).

Begin to understand percentages

Percentages are the third way of representing numbers between 0 and 1 (and bigger than 1 as pupils often do not realise that 200% is 2×). Work from 100% as 1, through 50% as $\frac{1}{2}$ and 0.50, 25% as $\frac{1}{4}$ and 0.25, 10% as $\frac{1}{10}$ and 0.10 to 1% being $\frac{1}{100}$ of something (some pupils may need a brief revision of dividing by 10 and 100). If a pupil can understand that 1% is $\frac{1}{100}$ and that it is obtained by dividing by 100 and that 2% is obtained by multiplying 1% value by 2, that 3% is by multiplying by 3, that 4%, etc., then she has the foundation for calculating percentages by formula. Fill in gaps of the easy values by discussion such as where will 20% go? What fraction and decimal is it equivalent to? Is it twice 10%? Is 5% half of 10%? Do some simple calculations on '25% of' by halving 50% and do 5% by halving 10%. Combine 25% and 50% to make 75% and 5% and 10% to make 15%. A 100 number square is good for visualising percentage values.

Calculations

Rapid recall of addition and subtraction facts

There will be some pupils for whom the task of rapid recall will be difficult. The additional pressure of responding quickly will exacerbate their problem. It will be vital for these pupils and helpful for the others if the connections and patterns are explained. The key number bonds for 10 can be extended to the decimal equivalents such as 0.2 + 0.8. Extension to examples such as:

> 6.2 + 3.8
> 37 + 63   and
> 450 + 550

may require a good visual image, possibly based on addition facts to 9 followed by addition facts to 10, for example,

- 6.2 + 3.8 is in two parts, whole numbers which add to 9 and decimals which add to 1.
- 37 + 63 is in two parts, tens which add to 90 and units which add to 10.
- 450 + 550 is in two parts, hundreds which add to 900 and tens which add to 100.

The visual image for number bonds for 100 could be money. So, for example, splitting 100 into two parts could be shown by trading a £1 coin, 100p for ten 10p coins. These can be divided into two lots, demonstrating the number bonds for ten extended to 100. The pattern written on the board, maybe as shown in Figure 3.1.

A second level of splitting up the 100 is then shown by taking one 10p coin and trading it for ten 1p coins (the tradings are reinforcing the concept of decomposition), so that there are now nine 10p coins and ten 1p coins, making 100. The two lots of coins can now be split, first the nine 10ps then the ten 1ps and the process discussed.

This is easily extended to decimals (ones and tenths) adding to 10.

This section provides good opportunities to build on and extend from key basic facts and thus help pupils understand the inter-relationships of numbers, which is an essential skill for mental arithmetic.

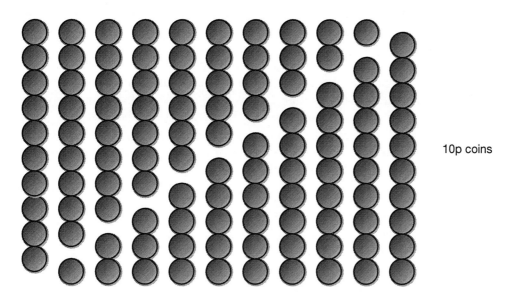

10p coins

Figure 3.1 Using 10p coins as images for number bonds for 100

Mental calculation strategies (+ and −)

This section builds on the previous section and relies very much on those skills being securely fixed in the pupils' memory . . . and retrievable from memory.

In addition to having good access to basic facts, pupils should be aware of and use the relationship between the four operations. This section focuses on the relationship between addition and subtraction and pupils will benefit from some simple demonstrations with the number line, moving forward for addition and backwards for subtraction and then discussing the significance of the difference between two numbers and the alternative subtraction procedure of counting on, emphasising the stepwise nature of this through, for example 10s and 100s (which we old folk used to do when counting on change). An example is 1000 − 648, where 648 is the start point.

$$648 + 2 = 650 \ldots 650 + 50 = 700 \ldots 700 + 300 = 1000 \ldots \text{answer } 352$$

Written addition (and subtraction) is traditionally done from right to left, from units digits to tens, hundreds and so on. If this is transferred to mental addition, then the answer is generated in reverse order, that is the unit digit is calculated first, but stated last in the digits that make up the answer. If pupils add from right to left, starting with the highest place values first, then they can repeat the digits of the answer as they construct the answer, in the correct order. For example, adding 425 and 367 could start at 400 + 300 = 700, then 20 + 60 = 80, taking the answer to 780, then 5 + 7 = 12, taking the answer to 792.

There may well be a need to develop appropriate flexibility in approaches for addition and subtraction, not least to recognise that there will be different cognitive styles within a class (back to the inchworms and grasshoppers).

A mental arithmetic skill that is easy to learn applies to numbers which are close to 10s, 100s, 1000s. For example 9 + 7 is 10 + 7 − 1 and 98 + 78 is 100 + 78 − 2 and 2993 + 88 is 3000 + 88 − 7 (any of these could be done in another order 88 − 7 + 3000). The same principle applies to subtraction. The most likely confusion is that the pupil will do the wrong adjustment, so in 98 + 78, they might add 2 instead of subtracting 2. This is an indication that number values and relationships are not well understood. The question 'Is the answer bigger, smaller or the same?' is useful yet again as a first estimate and check. A second check is knowing that 8 + 8 gives a unit digit of 6. Learning checking strategies is essential for accurate mental arithmetic.

Pencil and paper procedures (+ and −)

The Numeracy Strategy uses this section to reinforce mental arithmetic methods by encouraging pupils to document procedures other than just the traditional algorithm (procedure). There will be some pupils who compute so rapidly and intuitively that documentation will not be easy for them. A classroom ethos which encourages different methods will help. On the other hand, there will be pupils who will be confused by exposure to too many alternatives . . . the teacher's knowledge of an individual pupil's learning styles will enable him or her to balance and manage this.

'Carrying' and 'decomposition' (two words against which I have a personal vendetta) are essential procedures to understand. They are complementary and can be demonstrated together which may well reinforce the understanding that, like subtraction and addition being opposite versions of the same procedure, these two contributors to the procedures are also equal opposites.

The similarity can be demonstrated with coins or base ten blocks. I marginally prefer coins with this age group as they have some reality and the trading is common sense. So, set up an addition with coins and written numbers, say 57 + 78. Add the 1p coins to obtain 15p. Trade ten 1p coins for one 10p coin and 'carry' it to the tens column. Now add five 10p coins to seven 10p coins and the carried 10p coin to make thirteen 10p coins. Trade ten 10p coins for one pound coin (100) and 'carry' it to the hundreds column . . . answer 135.

Now subtract 78 from 135, which will require trading in the £1 coin for ten 10p coins and trading a 10p coin for ten 1p coins . . . decomposing the 100 + 30 + 5 to 120 + 15. Do some other examples. This should show the relationship between carrying and decomposition. The coin procedure mirrors the traditional written procedure.[1]

Understanding multiplication and division

The four operations, +, −, × and ÷ are closely inter-related. A clear understanding of each operation and how it relates to the others will strengthen the understanding of the other operations. Multiplication is often described as 'repeated addition' but the understanding of this phrase may not be clear. Similarly, division can be described as 'repeated subtraction'. Pupils will need some concrete material experiences to start to develop these concepts. The symbols will not be enough.

The basic ideas in this section are the commutative property of multiplication (8 × 7 = 7 × 8), the distributive law {23 × 45 = (20 + 3) × 45 = (20 × 45) + (3 × 45)}, the non-commutative nature of division and that division is the inverse of multiplication.

The connection between addition and multiplication can be explained (and linked back to earlier work and developed into new work) by starting with times table facts. So 3 × 6 is also 6 + 6 + 6. This can be sub-divided as (6 + 6) + 6 or (2 × 6) + 6, thereby introducing brackets. Similarly, 7 × 8 is also 8 + 8 + 8 + 8 + 8 + 8 + 8, which can be sub-divided as (8 + 8 + 8 + 8 + 8) + (8 + 8) or (5 × 8) + (2 × 8). This idea can be extended to a two digit multiplier such as 12 × 4 which is also 4 + 4 + 4 + 4 + 4 + 4 + 4 + 4 + 4 + 4 + 4 + 4 or (10 × 4) + (2 × 4). This then leads into the traditional written method for multiplications such as 46 × 51, which is calculated as (40 × 51) + (6 × 51) or as (50 × 46) + (1 × 46) which is the distributive law.

In each example of multiplication it is good to point out the division implications. For example 46 × 51 = 2346 should also be presented as 'How many 51s in 2346? What is 2346 divided by 51?'

Area is a good visual aid which can also give support to estimation of answers. This can be presented with base ten blocks and/or squared paper and later with just sketches of rectangles (see Figure 3.2).

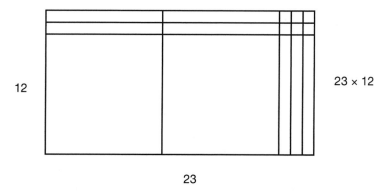

12

23 × 12

23

Figure 3.2 Base ten blocks used to show 23 × 12

Rapid recall of multiplication and division facts

The Strategy requires, as a key objective that pupils in Year 5 'Know by heart all multiplication facts up to 10 × 10.' Sadly, there will be a percentage of pupils who do not achieve this objective either because they do not practise enough, for which there is a potential solution, or because they just can't learn the facts, which requires a different solution and a degree of compromise and empathy. (My hypothesis is that some pupils have so often given a wrong answer, and probably not a consistently wrong answer, that the memory has not experienced an adequate and consistent input of correct information.) This situation will probably generate maths anxiety, greatly exacerbated by the additional need for 'rapid recall' and put a significant number of pupils into the 25 per cent who fail to reach the required standards. It seems inefficient to let this happen, since an inability to learn these facts does not preclude success as a mathematician. Your classroom management of this objective will have a profound effect on your statistics.

Some pupils will find this section merely another rote learning task at which, with some effort, they can succeed. There is a possibility that successful rote learning may reduce the need to understand and relate numbers. Thus all pupils should benefit from work which is built around patterns, consistent procedures and the inter-relationships between numbers.

For times table facts focus on what most can learn, $\times 0$, $\times 1$, $\times 2$, $\times 5$, $\times 10$. Build on these. A table square as opposed to separate times tables has the benefits of showing all the information at one go (gives the whole picture) and can be used for division as well as multiplication.

One of the useful strategies that pupils may adopt is the breaking down of numbers into easier chunks. For example, half of 920 might look daunting, but half of 800 plus half of 120 may be easier for some. While $800 + 120$ is a more creative split than the place value split of $900 + 20$ (this idea also supports a broader understanding of decomposition).

Many pupils read numbers literally. For example 9 is 9, the number after 8 rather than 1 less than 10. Twenty-five is only seen as a number in the twenties, not as $\frac{1}{4}$ of 100 or $\frac{1}{2}$ of 50 or even as $20 + 5$. Ninety-eight is seen as nine tens and eight units and not as 2 less than 100. Can your pupils learn to find the easy number breakdown? This is a very useful mental arithmetic skill and several worksheets deal with this area. As ever, visual images will help many pupils. For example a 100 square may help pupils see the closeness of numbers in the nineties to 100. Coins could also be used. One hundred 1p coins show the closeness of, say 96 to 100.

Mental calculation strategies ($\times$ and $\div$)

This should build on the foundations set up in the last section. Written procedures often require too much short term memory to be used for mental calculations, so different procedures need to be developed. Often these are based on the compensatory strategies some pupils use to circumvent their weak knowledge of basic facts.

There is more focus on multiplication than division in this section. The main learning points are again based on the inter-relationships of numbers. For example, to multiply by 6 you can multiply by factors 2 and then 3 ($6 = 2 \times 3$), to multiply by 50 you can multiply by 100 then divide by 2 ($50 = 100 \div 2$), to multiply by 12 you can multiply the number by 10, multiply the number by 2 and then add the two (partial) products together ($12 = 10 + 2$). Each time the operations follow the relationship used to separate the number, so for $\times 20$ you can use $\times 2$ and then $\times 10$ because $20 = 2 \times 10$ and for $\times 15$ you can use $\times 10$ plus $\times 5$ because $15 = 10 + 5$ (and $5\times$ can be obtained by halving $10\times$).

So this section uses the principle of converting one difficult step to (usually) two easier steps.

Look critically at some of the examples in Part 6 of the National Numeracy Strategy folder. It does not always use efficient number breakdowns. For example, it builds up a set of $\times 25$ facts by repeated doubling, giving 2×25, 4×25, 8×25, 16×25 and so on. An alternative set of facts would be 2×25, possibly

4×25, 10×25 and thus back to 5×25, then onto 20×25, 50×25, 100×25 and so on. This builds a better pattern and revisits the effect of multiples of 10, 100. Using these multiples means that 25×25 could be done as $(20 \times 25) + (5 \times 25)$ rather than $(16 \times 25) + (8 \times 25) + (1 \times 25)$.

Pencil and paper procedures ($\times$ and $\div$)

Approximations for TU $\times$ TU are helped by reviewing the area model for multiplication. Some examples are given below (see Figures 3.3 and 3.4).

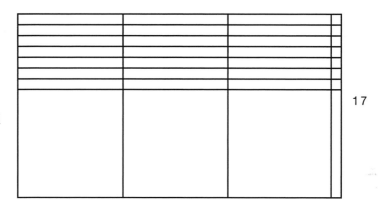

31×17 can be seen, as a first estimation to be over 300, just by counting the hundred squares. A second look would suggest an answer closer to 600.

17

31

Figure 3.3 Area model for 31 $\times$ 17

28×39 can be seen in comparison to 30×40, giving an estimate of less than 1200.

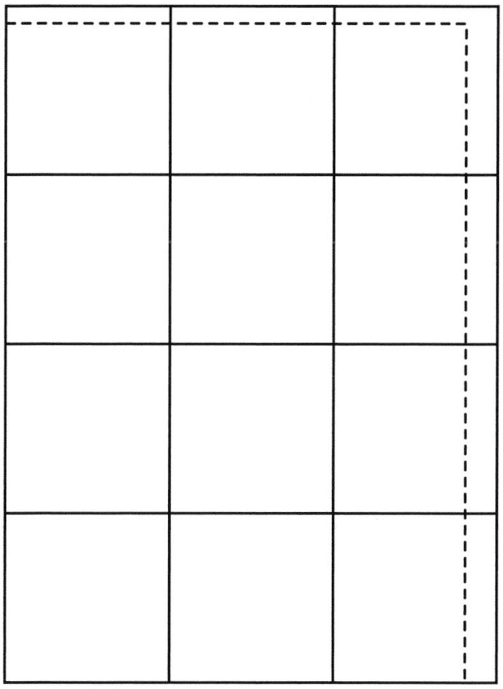

Figure 3.4 28 $\times$ 39 compared to 30 $\times$ 40 as areas

The area model also acts as a good illustration of partition methods. It also emphasises the units, tens and hundreds.

The long multiplication procedure is likely to be one of the first procedural barriers for pupils. It can be very abstract so memory has less chance of a 'realistic hook' to hang from and the organisation of the various written stages, including the 'carried' numbers is challenging. The area model, shown in base ten blocks, or on squared paper or just as sketched rectangles shows where each part of the calculation originates. The area model is also valuable in fractions and algebra. This means the pupils are getting a consistent and developmental image. If you start with the area and one side, division leads to finding the value of the other side. The same image, of course, works for multiplication and division and shows the inverse relationship between these two operations (see Figure 3.5).

Division by repeated (chunked) subtraction is the inverse of multiplication by partition. It can also be shown on the area model.

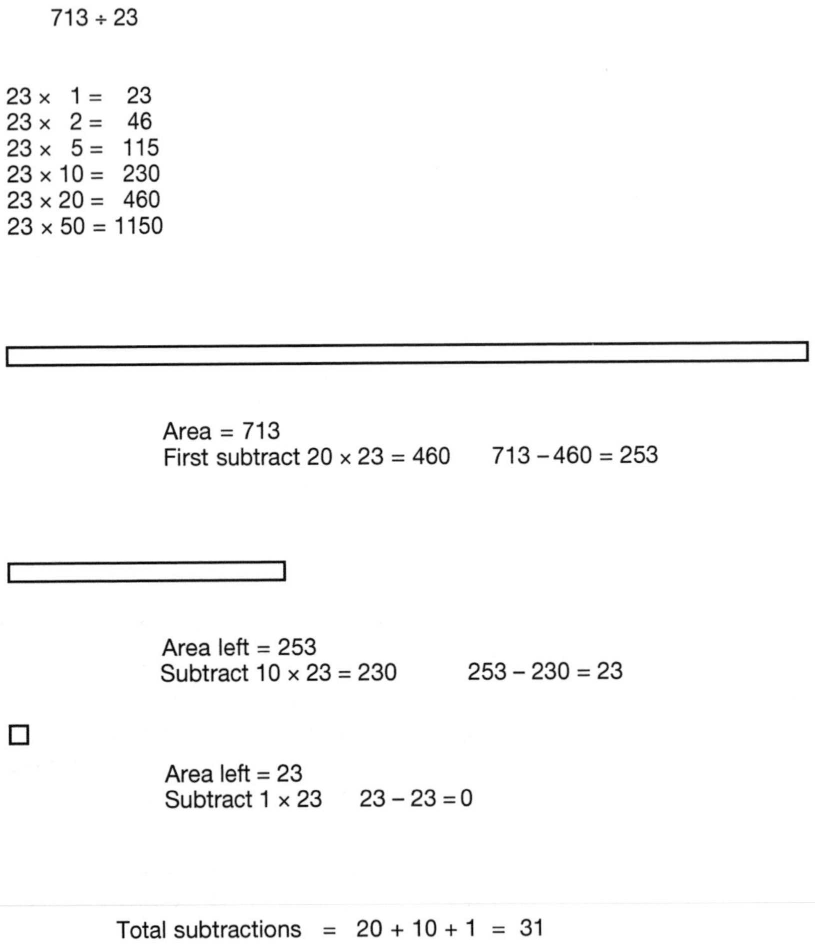

$$713 \div 23$$

$$
\begin{aligned}
23 \times 1 &= 23 \\
23 \times 2 &= 46 \\
23 \times 5 &= 115 \\
23 \times 10 &= 230 \\
23 \times 20 &= 460 \\
23 \times 50 &= 1150
\end{aligned}
$$

Area = 713
First subtract $20 \times 23 = 460$ $713 - 460 = 253$

Area left = 253
Subtract $10 \times 23 = 230$ $253 - 230 = 23$

Area left = 23
Subtract 1×23 $23 - 23 = 0$

Total subtractions $= 20 + 10 + 1 = 31$

Figure 3.5 Division by subtraction of 'chunks'

I like the values used in setting up key multiplication values, that is $1\times$, $2\times$, $5\times$, $10\times$, $20\times$, $50\times$, $100\times$ and so on along this pattern. So, for example, to divide 537 by 8, set up the table, using the patterns

$$1 \times 8 = 8$$
$$2 \times 8 = 16$$
$$5 \times 8 = 40$$
$$10 \times 8 = 80$$
$$20 \times 8 = 160$$
$$50 \times 8 = 400$$
$$100 \times 8 = 800$$

The answer to $537 \div 8$ can be seen to lie between 50 and 100, closer to 50, and a little less than 70 (50 + 20). Subtraction of multiples will take the pupil to an answer.

$$
\begin{array}{rl}
537 & \\
-400 & \quad 50 \times 8 \\
\hline
137 & \\
-80 & \quad 10 \times 8 \\
\hline
57 & \\
-40 & \quad 5 \times 8 \\
\hline
17 & \\
-16 & \quad 2 \times 8 \\
\hline
1 & \quad \text{answer : 67 remainder 1}
\end{array}
$$

This does relate to the standard written method. Both are by step by step subtraction of multiples of (in this case) 8.

Using a calculator

The requirement to calculate at speed will create errors for some pupils. Word questions in particular need to be carefully read right through to make sure the correct operation is chosen. Read these two examples carefully:

Question 1   Mark has 6 apples. James has 5 more apples than Mark. How many apples does James have?

Question 2   Mark has 6 apples. Mark has 5 more apples than James. How many apples does James have?

Both questions use the word 'more' which is usually associated with add, but question 1 could be written as $6 + 5 = 11$ and question 2 could be written as $6 - 5 = 1$. The wording of the two questions is extremely similar and both use 'more'.

Also look out for division and subtraction questions, where the words are often written in the opposite order to that needed for keying into the calculator, for example, 'Divide 6 into 48' or 'Subtract 15 from 32'. Remember to revise the fact that division and subtraction are not commutative.

Other classic errors are created by mixing units such as cm and m, or kg and g, and by mixing pence and pounds as in £47.60 − 45p (answered incorrectly as £2.60).

Checking the results of calculations

Another way of checking the addition of several numbers is to identify the combinations which make 10. For example look at the units column;

$$
\begin{array}{r}
46 \\
31 \\
87 \\
44 \\
33 \\
89 \\
+78 \\
\hline
\end{array}
$$

There are '10 combinations' in the units column, $6 + 4$, $1 + 9$, $7 + 3$. With the unmatched 8, this makes a total of 38. This procedure also practises number bonds for ten. Some pupils may introduce more sophisticated number combinations, such as $8 + 7 + 5 = 20$.

Another method of adding down a column of numbers is to use tallies. This method helps pupils with poorer short term memories. So, with the example above, as you add down the units column, $6 + 1 = 7$, $7 + 7 = 14$. Put a stroke through the 7 to mark the ten from the 14 and just move on with 4. So $4 + 4 = 8$, $8 + 3 = 11$. Put a stroke through the 3 to note the ten from the 11 and move on down with the 1 unit. $1 + 9 = 10$. Put a stroke through the 9 to mark another ten. 0 is added to 8, 8 goes in the units place of the answer column. There are three ten tallies, so 30 carries over to the tens column as 3 tens.

Checking calculations is usually most effective when a different method is used for the check. Pupils who have flexible approaches to procedures are likely to be much better at checking and evaluating their answers. Flexible thinking styles are explained in Chapter 4.

Solving problems

Making decisions

Some problems could be presented where the pupils are not actually required to work out the answer. For example, they could be asked to estimate an answer. This could be as basic as 'Is it bigger?' 'Is it smaller?' Pupils could be asked which operation they would use, +, −, × or ÷ and to explain how. This could also lead to useful discussions and comparisons of methods. The vocabulary around the four operations is varied in content and interpretation. The English language provides several ways of inferring add, subtract, multiply and divide. There is also the use of the same 'trigger' word to infer different operations (see 'Using a calculator'). This topic needs some careful examples and explicit instruction.

Making up 'number stories' is an important activity. Too often teachers expect pupils to 'translate' word problems into mathematical equations/statements whilst forgetting the reverse translation. By doing this pupils can learn how word problems are constructed (usually resulting in totally boring, anorak questions in text books) and how misleading features can be introduced, such as extraneous data. It can also be fun and creative!

Making up number stories can help pupils understand how key words can be used to mean different operations and move them away from an overly literal interpretation of vocabulary. (See Chapter 6.)

Reasoning and generalising about numbers or shapes

It is not always easy for a pupil to explain their reasoning for a mental calculation. It will help this objective if the classroom ethos is open and flexible. Even then some pupils may find that their method is so intuitive (and quick) that they cannot really explain all that happened in the brain. This may improve as pupils become accustomed to the idea of analysing their thinking.

Of course, once a teacher knows the procedure used by a pupil, she or he might be tempted to suggest changes or alternatives. This may not always be the best move and instant change may well not be possible for the pupil. This whole area of cognitive style is fascinating and important. Ideally pupils should learn to be flexible in their choice of methods (and, hopefully appropriate to their own sub-skills), being able to use successfully a range of procedures. For most pupils this will happen over a period of time of exposure to the idea and encouragement to work in this more open manner. It must not be assumed that pupils can adjust their cognitive style overnight. (For more details on thinking style see Chapter 4.)

This topic area can be used to develop further flexibility in using numbers and to show the inter-relationships, especially those which make the manipulation of numbers easier, for example 49×30 calculated via 50×30.

Spatial examples can be a break from number crunching activities and may well allow some pupils who have strong spatial skills to succeed.

Equally unstructured questions of the type $t + h + w = 1$ will confuse some pupils. Some will just not have the confidence or skill to actually start the process, even with encouragement. Be prepared to lead more than you might want!

Angle work enters a new world where a key value is 90, not 100 and where the length of the two lines which meet to make an angle do not effect the size/value of the angle.

There are ample examples of angles around us in everyday life which can be used to set the picture for this section. Again it is possible to build on what the pupil knows, but may not have internalised or related. Right angles abound and it is easy to show aspects of two, three and four right angles. A clock face is a good source for 360°, 30°, 90°, 180°, 270° and so on. A square shows 45°. Make sure the pupils have a sound foundation on which to build their concepts.

Problems involving 'real life', money and measures

The Numeracy Strategy provides ample opportunity for reviews, revisits and revision. This overlearning is a strong positive factor in the acquisition of numeracy skills. Additionally, the interlinking of different sections can be used to help develop and consolidate concepts.

So word problems occur again giving another chance to explore the meaning and uses of mathematical vocabulary.

This section allows teachers to introduce some truly 'real life' work, such as money, exchange rates and measures. It would seem an ideal section in which to use manipulative materials such as coins, bottles, scales and such. Let pupils experience 100 g, 100 ml and see everyday recognisable examples to give them a basis for judging their answers in this area.

For foreign exchange it would be good to have some foreign currency, and possibly discuss which values of coins and notes are chosen and why. (For example, the UK works on 1, 2, 5, 10, 20, 50, 100, etc.)

When dealing with recipes, talk about the reality of proportions when calculations may lead to $5\frac{1}{2}$ eggs. Perhaps do some costing for recipes.

With questions on time, remind pupils that for time 60 and 12 are the key numbers. Practise counting through a minute and an hour (58 seconds, 59 seconds, 60 seconds . . . 1 minute, and 58 minutes, 59 minutes, 60 minutes . . . 1 hour).

There can be some conceptual problems with the 24 hour clock. The two most likely confusions are with 20:00 hours (8 p.m.) and 22:00 hours (10 p.m.), so try to pre-empt the difficulty. The clock is now the only base 12 experience children will have.

Handling data

Probability

This is a topic which lends itself to discussion around events which are within a pupil's experience and from which the mathematical groundwork can be naturally derived. Probability is 'everyday', covering topics such as the chance that it will rain to the probability of it being an 'Eastenders' night.

It allows involvement of all pupils and is an area of maths which, at this stage, is not a matter of producing an exact answer to be correct. In this introductory stage, pupils can get a feel of probability values (and perhaps a more rational understanding of risks that are often overstated). As ever, it allows for some cross linking to other topics. For example, an understanding of fractions may be improved when considering probabilities such as $\frac{1}{50}$ compared to $\frac{1}{10}$.

Organising and interpreting data

Collecting and classifying data is usually a less stressful and less judgmental activity. With careful instruction all pupils should produce acceptable work in this area. The word frequency may cause some confusion and needs good and clear definition.

There is good computer software which prints out charts, giving an opportunity to discuss the clarity and appropriateness of presentation. This can also circumvent the drawing problems some pupils may exhibit (for example, dyspraxic pupils). Alternatively, pupils could be given support by supplying a partially completed graph, say with the axes already drawn and labelled, or a data sheet with the chart already drawn and ready for the pupil to use for her collection of data.

There are sets of data that can be collected which allow the involvement of all pupils, for example, the colours of cars or vans passing by the school, the heights of pupils, shoe sizes, dates of birth (i.e. the day of the month), particular words in a newspaper, comics/magazines, popular sweets and so on.

For line graphs pupils need to know the significance of starting an axis at a value other than zero (and how this can distort the relative values of data – a qualitative link to proportion). The labelling of axes is another habit that pupils need to acquire.

This section also acts as an early experience of averages as a 'central' measure and an opportunity to evaluate data objectively. This should again give good opportunity for realistic inclusion.

Measures, shape and space

The shape and space section could show up a new group of pupils who have strengths in maths and another group which find these concepts more difficult.

Measures

This section allows ample scope to work on pupils' existing experiences and bring together experiences to create understandings and concepts. For example, pupils know the standard soft drink can size and can be shown that this is close to $\frac{1}{3}$ of a litre. This fraction can then be shown in terms of cl and ml. The contents of a can can be measured exactly and the result used for discussion on averages and the place of precise and approximate measurements in everyday life. The new work can be built around everyday experience and previous numeracy knowledge, combining revision and awareness to develop understanding.

The metric prefixes of m, c, d, and k are not always perceived to be consistent. This may in part be due to the kilogram, which is an anomaly compared to the metre and the litre. Also, the kilometre is often viewed as a separate unit to the metre, since the scale and use of this unit is not necessarily connected to the relatively small scale, everyday sized metre. These areas may well need to be addressed explicitly. It is both important and extremely useful to know that the metric prefixes are consistent. (I do feel that examiners and writers of exercise/text books sometimes inadvertently exacerbate this problem by setting deliberately confusing questions.)

The confusions which might arise in this section can be reduced by using the ample opportunities available to show real items which relate the theory to experience and give pupils a baseline image for measures.

Reading from scales is an important, cross curriculum skill and estimating a reading which falls between divisions is a good estimation skill which relates back to 'Numbers and the Number System'. Using a large scale (that is with big distances between divisions) should help. Circular and curved scales should also be demonstrated. (This also offers some revision of proportion.)

Areas may need a fundamental revision before moving to the new work. It always impresses me that 7×7 is an area very close to half of 10×10. This shift in comparison parameters is demanding and may well be helped by building up some 'easy' areas with unifix cubes or similar.

Basic reference values, such as $100 \text{ mm}^2 = 1 \text{ cm}^2$ and $10,000 \text{ cm}^2 = 1 \text{ m}^2$ need to be acceptable as well as remembered.

Perimeter and area can be confused during calculations, so it is helpful to establish a clear picture in pupils' minds for each word. A simple link such as perimeter *fence* (which infers a line) may suffice. It is also useful to emphasise the units used and to create a visual image of a square centimetre and a square metre.

Reading from timetables requires tracking skills. Pupils who do not have this skill will need structured, small step instruction to learn the skill. An L-shaped piece of card may help with the actual process of tracking. A possible practise topic is a number square or times table square. Most rail companies have summary timetables giving only two or three destinations (for example there is a timetable for just Exeter, Taunton and London). These offer easier tracking tasks.

Shape and space

The language content around shapes is quite complex. There are some benefits in words like scalene and isosceles in the sense that they are not used in other contexts and with other meanings. There is a considerable new vocabulary to learn and some help may be needed, for example explaining that 'iso' means same and that 'octo' refers to eight as in octopus.

Some children will find two dimensional representations of three dimensional shapes difficult. Explicit instruction, based on real shapes should help.

For coordinates, the most likely error will be in mixing up x and y coordinates. The simple mnemonic 'along the corridor (x) and up the stairs (y)' may help give the correct order.

Angle values, as with any values, need a reference example which is automatised. For angles the most likely value is 90° and from this can be derived (and visualised) 45°, 30°, 60°, 10°, 110°, 135°, 150° and so on. Work on complementary angles (adding to 180°) provides a little revision of subtraction and addition skills and on recognising the closeness of 90 to 100 and 180 to 200.

Shape and space is a visual topic and must be accompanied by visual teaching materials. Development of this skill is via hands-on materials, for example pupils should have nets which they can handle and shape before they advance to doing this purely by visualising.

Chapter 4

Thinking styles in mathematics

Introduction

The designers of mathematics curricula across the world seem to be moving to some similar conclusions. One of which is that the curriculum must encourage flexible thinking. Presumably this is to encourage good problem solving skills to complement good computational skills.

Formulas, procedures and accurate and swift recall of facts will lead to success in number work, but countries need problem solvers as well as computationally adept pupils (particularly when calculators and computers are readily available).

Two thinking styles

Several researchers have suggested that there are two styles of thinking for mathematics, extremes at the ends of a continuum. Ideally learners should be able to move appropriately between styles as they solve problems. Two American colleagues and I studied thinking styles, which they had labelled 'inchworm' and 'grasshopper'. Grasshoppers are holistic, intuitive and resist documenting methods. Inchworms are formulaic, procedural, sequential and need to document. The two styles are described and compared in Table 4.1.

M.R. Marolda and P.S. Davidson, researchers from the USA, also tabulated (Table 4.2) the characteristics of what they call Mathematics Learning Style I (similar to the inchworm) and Mathematics Learning Style II (similar to the grasshopper).[1] By describing learning style as opposed to thinking style they take in a broader picture, but describe similar patterns to those in Table 4.1.

The impact of this construct is often under-rated. It seems obvious that the way that learners think will be a very critical factor in the way they learn and in the way they are taught.

The three examples below illustrate thinking styles in operation.

Table 4.1 Thinking styles of the inchworm and the grasshopper

	Inchworm	Grasshopper
First approach to a problem	1 Focuses on the parts and details.	1 Overviews, holistic, puts together.
	2 Looks at the numbers and facts to select a suitable formula or procedure.	2 Looks at the numbers and facts to estimate an answer, or narrow down the range of answers. Controlled exploration.
Solving the problem	3 Formula, procedure-oriented	3 Answer-oriented.
	4 Constrained focus. Uses one method.	4 Flexible focus. Uses a range of methods.
	5 Works in serially ordered steps, usually forward.	5 Often works back from a trial answer.
	6 Uses numbers exactly as given.	6 Adjusts, breaks down/builds up numbers to make an easier calculation.
	7 More comfortable with paper and pen. Documents method.	7 Rarely documents method. Performs calculations mentally (and intuitively).
Checking and evaluating answers	8 Unlikely to check or evaluate answer. If a check is done it will be by the same procedure/ method.	8 Likely to appraise and evaluate answer against original estimate. Checks by an alternative method/ procedure.
	9 Often does not understand procedures or values of numbers. Works mechanically.	9 Good understanding of number, methods and relationships.

Thinking style and computation

Thinking style will influence how a learner uses numbers and the operations (+, −, ×, ÷).

Inchworms see numbers and the symbols for operations literally. In the example below, 98 is seen as just 98, not as a number very close to 100. Indeed if you ask an inchworm to adjust 98 to an easier number they may not relate to the question and if they do try to answer they may well say 96. They will go into subtraction mode applying the subtraction rules automatically, probably with little or no understanding of the maths behind the procedure (Figure 4.1).

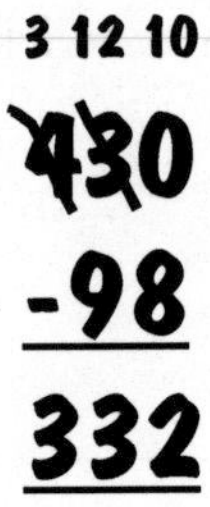

$$
\begin{array}{r}
\scriptstyle 3\ 12\ 10 \\
\cancel{4}\cancel{3}0 \\
-\ 98 \\
\hline
332
\end{array}
$$

Figure 4.1 Subtraction the inchworm way

Table 4.2 Mathematics learning styles I and II

Mathematics Learning Style I	Mathematics Learning Style II
Highly reliant on verbal skills.	Prefers perceptual stimuli and often reinterprets abstract situations visually or pictorially.
Tends to focus on individual details or single aspects of a situation.	Likes to deal with big ideas; doesn't want to be bothered with the details.
Sees the 'trees', but overlooks the 'forest'.	
Prefers HOW to WHY.	Prefers WHY to HOW.
Relies on a preferred sequence of steps to pursue a goal.	Prefers non-sequential approaches involving patterns and interrelationships.
Reliant on teacher for THE approach.	
Lack of versatility.	
Challenged by perceptual demands.	Challenged by demands for details or the requirement for precise solutions.
Prefers quizzes or unit tests to more comprehensive final exams.	Prefers performance based or portfolio type assessments to typical tests.
	More comfortable recognising correct solutions than generating them.
	Prefers comprehensive exams.

If the question had been asked as mental arithmetic, then the load on short term memory and visualising the process in the mind would be significant. If the learner has those skills then the method is acceptable even if not efficient.

The grasshopper will use his good sense of number values and the interrelationship of operations.

◆ The 98 will be rounded up to 100 (by adding 2);
◆ The (simple) subtraction 430 − 100 gives 330;
◆ The grasshopper knows that this intermediate answer is smaller than the correct answer (by 2);
◆ Adding 2 takes him to the correct answer of 332.

The load on short term memory is less. There is less need to visualise the process in your mind. The method uses good awareness of number values.

Thinking style and problem solving

Question   Which stall at a fair raises £90, if the total raised is £500 and

tombola takes   34%
books takes   11%
cakes takes   23%
spinner takes   18%
crafts takes   14%   of the total?

An inchworm methodically calculates, starting at the top of the list

$$\frac{34}{100} \times £500 = £170$$

$$\frac{11}{100} \times £500 = £55$$

$$\frac{23}{100} \times £500 = £115$$

$$\frac{18}{100} \times £500 = £90$$

A grasshopper looks at the same question and writes 18%, the spinner. The teacher asks 'Where is your working out?' *'Didn't do any'* 'So how did you do it?' *'Just knew.'* 'No working, no marks.' How the grasshopper did the question was to overview all the percentages and see that among the percentages, only one was a multiple of nine. Eighteen is a multiple of nine, so 18% must be the answer. Is that explanation acceptable, even if documented?

Thinking style and shape and space problems

What is the area of the shaded part of Figure 4.2? (A written answer, with method is expected, or a verbal explanation.)

An inchworm with few mathematical skills may well simply count the squares. A more mathematically sophisticated inchworm will analyse the *parts* of the figure, seeing a triangle, a square and two thin rectangles. Then, if he brings a knowledge of area to the problem he may well calculate the area of the triangle from the formula $\frac{1}{2} \times$ base $\times$ height and thus onto the square and the 'legs'.

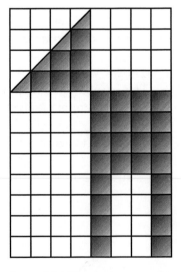

Figure 4.2 What is the area of the shaded figure?

Head/triangle area $= \frac{1}{2} \times 4 \times 4 = 8$
Body/square area $= 4 \times 4 = 16$ subtotal 24
leg 1 area $= 4$ subtotal 28
leg 2 area $= 4$ *total 32*

The addition of the area of each part is likely to be sequential and irrespective of any number bonds for ten, as in adding a leg to the body to make 20. Inchworms tend not to overview or, indeed look ahead.

On the positive side, the inchworm will be able to document his method, quote formulae and show that, even if he makes an error with the calculation, he has knowledge of area calculations.

The grasshopper may seek to redesign and simplify the problem. He will take a holistic view, trying to put the parts together, so the triangle is 'seen' as half of a 4×4 square. The gap between the two legs is also half of a 4×4 square, so the triangle can be used to fill that gap and make a 4×8 rectangle giving an area of 32. This method is far more difficult for the pupil to document.[2]

Thinking styles and the National Numeracy Strategy

There will be expectations with thinking style implications for pupils learning mathematics. A specific example is when learners are expected to be able to estimate answers to simple numerical calculations. A more general expectation is that pupils show flexibility in the way they handle mathematics.

The National Numeracy Strategy states a number of outcomes (which really are expectations) that pupils should achieve. Some of these are related to inchworm thinking and some to the grasshopper style of thinking. Krutetskii, a psychologist and mathematician specified flexibility of thinking as one of the key requisites for being a good mathematician. The National Council of Teachers of Mathematics (USA) also lists flexibility as one of the characteristics of good mathematicians. This requirement seems to me to have face validity, that is it just feels sensible and right. It is possible to survive maths as an inchworm, though there are a number of essential skills needed to make this an effective style, for example a good memory for sequential information. It is less likely that a grasshopper will survive school maths, especially at higher levels where documentation is essential, but it is likely he will be successful at 'life maths'. So ultimately it is not the end of the world if your maths thinking style is at either extreme, but in the school environment it will, inevitably, be more of a problem. As an adult who can usually avoid some maths, if not all maths, it is less critical that you are not a flexible thinker, but in general terms as a problem solver, it is going to be better if you can develop flexible thinking. So schools can help and, as ever, awareness of the implications of everything you teach and how you teach it is an important factor. It is back to 'What else are you teaching?'

The NNS encourages pupils to share their different methods and for teachers to present different methods. This will require good sales techniques. Some pupils will just not want to buy into different methods because they think one is enough and two or more will be confusing. Each method should illustrate another facet of number and, even if the pupil doesn't adopt the method, an exposure to a different way of perceiving a problem should be beneficial.

I have listed the outcomes that the NNS expects of pupils. Where the text is plain, the outcome is inchworm biased, when the text is italic, the outcome is more favourable to a grasshopper thinking style. Underlined text is not thinking style specific.

The NNS states that your pupils should:

♦ *have a sense of the size of a number and where it fits in the number system*;
♦ know by heart number facts such as number bonds (*10*), multiplication tables, *doubles and halves*;
♦ *use what they know by heart to figure out answers mentally*;
♦ calculate accurately and efficiently, both *mentally* and with paper and pen, *drawing on a range of calculation strategies*;
♦ explain their methods and reasoning using correct mathematical terms;
♦ *judge whether their answers are reasonable and have strategies for checking them where necessary*;
♦ recognise when it is appropriate to use a calculator and be able to do so effectively;
♦ *make sense of number problems, including non-routine problems*, and recognise the operations needed to solve them.

Some examples of methods advocated by the NNS that could be classified as grasshopper include:

♦ In Year 1 pupils are encouraged to explore all the pairs of numbers which add to 6.
♦ In Year 2 the mental addition $16 + 7$ is shown as $16 + 4 + 3$ and $22 - 7$ is $22 - 2 - 5 = 15$.
♦ In Year 3 the four times-table facts are obtained by doubling the two times-table facts.
♦ In Year 4 pupils practise responding rapidly to oral or written questions, *explaining the strategy used*. (Sadly there is still this need to do maths quickly, which is not so good for many dyslexics.)
♦ In Year 5 (continue) to add/subtract 9, 19, 29 . . . or 11, 21, 31. . . . by adding or subtracting 10, 20, 30 . . . then adjusting. A Year 5 pupil is taught to 'see' $1.5 + 1.6$ as double 1.5 plus 0.1.
♦ In Years 5 and 6 pupils are asked to find percentages by halving and quartering and halving again, as in finding 12.5% of £36 000 by halving three times and in finding 75% of £300 by halving to get 50%, halving again to get 25% and adding to obtain 75%. This is inter-relating numbers, building up and breaking down numbers.

Some examples from the NNS that could be classified as inchworm include;

♦ Knowing facts by heart in Year 1.
♦ In Year 2 find a small difference between a pair of numbers using counting.
♦ Using number lines for addition in Year 3.
♦ In Year 4 using standard written methods for short multiplication.
♦ Using standard written methods for addition and subtraction in Years 5 and 6.

The NNS advocates a mixture of thinking styles (without actually articulating this as a policy). Such implications exist in the curiculum statements of other countries, too, for example in Eire, the Mathematics Curriculum of 1999 is structured to 'enable the teacher to cater for individual differences in ability, previous learning and learning style.' While in Hong Kong, the curriculum includes:

> *Fostering general abilities and skills.* It is important that students need to develop their capabilities to learn how to learn, to think logically and creatively, to develop and use knowledge, to analyse and solve problems, to access information and process it effectively and to communicate with others so that they can meet the challenges that confront them now and in the future. Acquiring mathematics knowledge has always been emphasised, but fostering these general abilities and skills are strongly advocated for all students in the revised curriculum.

Can you change or influence thinking style?

First you have to ask 'Would it be a good idea?' Basically the wisdom for maths is that learners need to be able to draw on both thinking styles, maybe even in the course of solving a single question. Learners might start with the overviewing skills of the grasshopper, moving onto the documenting and procedural skills of the inchworm and finally checking the answer using the appraising skills of the grasshopper. Also some questions and topics lend themselves more to one thinking style. For example, mental arithmetic is better for grasshoppers, whilst algebra is more inchworm friendly. So the question becomes, can you teach learners to make appropriate use of both styles?

Returning for a moment to the first form of the question, a European study carried out with colleagues in the UK, Holland and Ireland showed that the design of the maths curriculum can have an influence on thinking style. It also showed that many learners can be taught flexible thinking, but, inevitably there will be those who are exceptions. There will be those whose thinking style is so fixed that they can only be taught in that dominant style. For example George was an extreme inchworm. As an eleven year old he would draw, with a ruler, large, complex and extremely detailed pictures of fantasy army vehicles. Despite more than four years of encouraging flexibility in his approach to maths we had to accept that he was a terminal inchworm. We taught him methods that acknowledged this and he achieved a Grade D in GCSE maths. Typical of his problem solving was a trial and adjust question:

Question   The formula $V = \dfrac{d^3}{2}$ gives the approximate volume of a sphere.

V is the volume in cm^3
d is the diameter in cm

A sphere has a volume of 120 cm^3.

Use trial and improvement to find the diameter, correct to 1 decimal place.

Use the table to record your trials. The first is done for you (see Figure 4.3).

d	V	
	too small	too large
5	**62.5**	
6		129.6
5.5	91.5	
5.6	98.3	
5.7	105.5	
5.8	113.1	
5.9	121.7	

Figure 4.3 Trial and adjust the inchworm way

As you can see George had a procedure, unfortunately not a numerically accurate one, which did not include evaluating each trial. He went straight to 6, saw the value he got for V was too big, but did not evaluate or appreciate how close this value of V was to the target answer of 120. He used his secure inchworm strategy – start in the middle, 5.5, and work up, which he did meticulously 0.1 at a time till he arrived (just as the space in the table was about to run out) at his answer, 5.9 cm.

So, the answer is 'Usually, yes, but not with everyone.' If you can you should. If you can't then you may do more harm than good and you should teach to the entrenched style. This decision may be linked to where the learner is in his educational career. If he is approaching GCSE then it is too late to try such a change. Impending examinations create different priorities.

During our European study on thinking style we asked pupils as they worked through questions which were designed to diagnose their thinking style, 'How did you do that?' and then a follow up question, 'Can you think of another way to do the question?' After six months in the school we retested and the percentage of pupils who could think of an alternative method had more than doubled. Now our hypothesis was not that the style of teaching was the main cause, though it does lead to increased flexibility over a longer period of time, but that it was mainly the ethos of the classroom which allowed pupils to explore different approaches. The work was done pre-NNS and the results may be different now. This key philosophy of the NNS seems to me to be one of the best components of its structure.

Finally, remember that the uncertain learner often likes the security of the familiar, even if the familiar is not all that successful. Teachers may have to do the hard sell on that alternative method.

How do you teach flexible thinking style?

The design of the curriculum is a great influence. If it actively encourages flexibility then most learners will adapt. If it dictates limited methods then most pupils will not explore alternatives. It is a classic example of the interaction between the cognitive and the affective domains.

The ethos of the classroom is another key factor. If learners are encouraged to explore different methods and their efforts are praised and appreciated (children are adept at spotting false praise) then they will generate a learning culture of flexible thinking. Like the CASE[3] and CAME[4] programmes I believe that thinking style teaching should be integrated into the curriculum rather than be taught as a separate skill.

So, as promoted by the NNS pupils can be encouraged to share and discuss different methods. There is a need to manage the extreme inchworms who may be confused by too much choice, but valuing different approaches will encourage flexibility. Once again the culture of speed may be counter-productive. If we are encouraging pupils to read, digest, analyse and comprehend questions then the pressure of speed may discourage them from doing that. It should be that there are set times and topics where a more reflective approach is encouraged.

Two key grasshopper skills an inchworm should adopt:

1   Inter-relating numbers, for example, seeing 9 as 1 less than 10, seeing 5 as half of 10.
2   Overviewing any problem, for example reading to the end before starting or getting a feel of what the answer may be.

Two key inchworm skills a grasshopper should adopt:

1   Explaining their methods.
2   Documenting their methods.

As a first example of teaching pupils to be flexible thinkers whilst acknowledging potential gaps in sub-skills, let's take a column addition. Take ten two digit numbers at random.

```
  23        Start by eliminating combinations of unit digits which add to 10
  51
  74        4 + 6 = 10
  99        1 + 9 = 10
  38
  12        8 + 2 = 10
  66
  42
  49
+ 85        5 + 3 + 2 = 10   just a 9 left, and a total of four tens (40)
 ───
   9
```

The same strategy is used for the tens digits.

This method:

♦ revises the number bonds for 10;
♦ reduces the risks of addition errors;
♦ reduces the load on short term memory;
♦ and consequently is low stress.

This method is more grasshopper style.

An alternative method, which is more towards the inchworm style is to use markers every time additions go above nine. So, as the units digits are added from top down,

$$3 + 1 = 4 \quad 4 + 4 = 8 \quad 8 + 9 = 17$$

a strike is put through the 9 to represent the 10 and the addition continues with the 7

$$7 + 8 = 15$$

so another strike is used, this time through the 8. The 5 is carried onwards

$$5 + 2 = 7 \quad 7 + 6 = 13$$

so another strike is used, this time through the 6. The 3 is carried onwards

$$3 + 2 = 5 \quad 5 + 9 = 14$$

so a fourth strike is used, this time through the 9. The 4 is carried onwards

$$4 + 5 = 9 \text{ which is written in the units total.}$$

There are four strikes, so 40 is carried as 4 tens into the tens column. The same procedure is then used for the tens column.

$$
\begin{array}{r}
23 \\
51 \\
74 \\
9\cancel{9} \\
3\cancel{8} \\
12 \\
\cancel{66} \\
42 \\
4\cancel{9} \\
+\ 85 \\
\hline
539
\end{array}
$$

This method:

♦ supports short term memory;
♦ avoids taking the pupil to any total beyond 19;
♦ is structured and sequential;
♦ and is more inchworm friendly.

The first method encourages pupils to scan down the numbers and spot the '10s'. The second method is more structured and is less likely to encourage any overview.

A good question to ask pupils and to support overviewing is to ask them to estimate a total. (There are ten numbers. If they span the range of 10 to 99 reasonably equally, then an acceptable average is 50 and an estimate is $50 \times 10 = 500$.

As a second example of teaching pupils to be flexible thinkers let's take a word problem about legs . . .

> *Question 1*   On a farm there is a total of 35 pigs and chickens. If the total number of legs for these pigs and chickens is 120, how many chickens are there on the farm?

A grasshopper will focus on the numbers involved, that is 35 and 120. The numbers suggest that the answer is likely to be a factor of 5 and there are likely to be more pigs. So try a 20/15 split (using a trial and adjust approach, but selecting numbers in a logically controlled way rather than just a random choice.

$20 \times 4 = 80$ $15 \times 2 = 30$

$60 + 30 = 110$

Since this is too few legs and 5 is the factor to consider, move to a 25/10 split to obtain more legs.

$25 \times 4 = 100$ $10 \times 2 = 20$ Total = 120

There may be no documentation or perhaps just a couple of scribbled numbers. The grasshopper needs to be encouraged to articulate his method and to make notes that communicate his thinking processes.

The inchworm with good algebra skills will set up simultaneous (that is, two) equations

p = number of pigs c = number of chickens

$p + c = 35$ (based on the number of creatures)

$4p + 2c = 120$ (based on the number of legs)

These will then be solved by substitution, say of $p = 35 - c$ into the second equation and the answers will be

$p = 25$ $c = 10$

The inchworm *may* substitute these answers back into the original question to check their accuracy.

The inchworm needs to be encouraged to make an initial appraisal and an estimate of an answer, even if it is just back at the 'Is the answer bigger or smaller?' which in this case is 'Are there more chickens or pigs?'

The grasshopper overview for Question 1 depended on 5 as a factor in the numbers involved. The other encouraging numbers are 1, 2 and 10. There may be a slightly different approach for Question 2.

> *Question 2*   There are a total of 42 pigs and chickens on a farm. If they have a total of 126 legs, how many are pigs?

The inchworm will again set up simultaneous equations. If he does not have this skill or the confidence to use this skill then he may try trial and adjust, but the choice of a starting number will be problematic and fairly random. It is unlikely to relate to an appraisal of the numbers in the question.

The grasshopper may well appreciate that the average number of legs for a pig and a chicken is 3 and that $3 \times 2 = 6$, so the number of pigs and chickens are the same (to give the average value of 3) and thus there are 21 of each creature.

If he doesn't sense the answer so precisely, he will still feel that the numbers are near and try the easy split of 22 and 20 and then adjust to 21/21.

If the question now uses 'unfriendly' numbers, then . . .

> *Question 3*   The number of pigs and the number of chickens on a farm add up to 39. The numbers of legs add up to 124. How many pigs are there?

The inchworm will use an algebra solution again. This is ideal for an inchworm, because he has been able to solve all three problems with the same method, if he has the requisite skills.

There are several trial and adjust style methods for a grasshopper to try. A grasshopper with a less sophisticated skill of controlled exploration may just start with 40 (easier to compute than 39).

$40 \times 4 = 160$ He can then adjust back to 39 pigs to obtain 156.

Now appraisal skills can be used to compare 156 with the target number of 124. A difference of 32 legs suggests there should be 16 chickens. (If one chicken is exchanged for one pig, there will be 2 less legs). Thus there are 23 pigs.

A grasshopper may split 39 into 19 and the easy number 20 (but still see the 19 as $20 - 1$).

Then a first trial gives

$$20 \times 4 = 80$$
$$19 \times 2 = 38$$
$$\overline{\text{Total} = 118}$$

'Is the answer smaller or bigger?' takes the grasshopper to add in more pigs. To reach the target number of 124, 6 more legs are needed so there must be 3 more pigs. Thus there are 23 pigs.

In each example the inchworm was able to use the same algebraic procedure. The grasshopper has used a version of trial and adjust, but has usually worked from an initial controlled estimate (that is, not a wild guess).

Do teachers have different thinking styles?

I have lectured to teachers about thinking style for many years and usually this involves asking the group to do some maths questions which can be used to diagnose thinking style. When I ask the group to decide which style predominates for each of them, the show of hands is almost always close to a 50/50 split. It's not sophisticated statistically, but by now it is a very large sample!

Another informal survey which was built into my lectures for about three years suggested that different teachers appraise the different styles of thinking of their pupils differently.

A Manchester Metropolitan University study showed that teachers who are not maths specialists but find themselves teaching maths may well regress, out of insecurity, to the formulaic methods they learnt at school, in the same way that insecure pupils do.

Teachers need to realistically appraise their own thinking style when teaching maths and appraising maths and look at the pupils who sail through their lessons. Then they should look at the pupils who struggle and see if a mismatch of thinking style is a contributing factor. The NNS guides teaches towards flexibility. (In fact it starts predominantly grasshopper and then gradually introduces more inchworm methods as the emphasis moves more towards written maths.)

The English exam system encourages documentation which puts grasshoppers at a disadvantage. Lack of documentation at A level may well result in failure, even if the answer is correct.

Encouraging flexible thinking style

Flexible thinking should permeate each lesson. Teaching this flexibility should begin at an early age. Some researchers state that thinking style is habitual, but my experience suggests that for many pupils (not all, as ever) thinking style is definitely open to influence. Curriculum can influence as we found in our tri-country study. I am pleased to see that the key requisites of the grasshopper style are set into the early years programmes of the NNS. There is a lot of content on inter-relating numbers and the four operations. Written methods and a more formulaic approach are gradually introduced as the curriculum progresses.

One of the other key lessons is to encourage learners to overview and review.

The old teaching adage of 'Tell 'em what you are going to teach, teach 'em, tell 'em what you've just taught them' could infer 'supply an introductory overview, provide a detailed explanation and then review and appraise the whole process and results.' You cover the cognitive styles and teach flexibility and thoroughness in working processes.

Different methods should be encouraged, valued and evaluated.

As an example of using different methods consider how the relationship of the numbers can affect the methods used when adding and subtracting. An inchworm will focus on the symbol (+ or −) and move to use a procedure irrespective of the numbers involved. For example faced with 600 − 594 an inchworm is likely to start decomposing (urgh!) rather than appreciate that the closeness of the two numbers takes him to an easy solution.

Flexible methods for mental addition and subtraction

In each case I have listed the essential sub-skills needed to succeed when using each method. This may help teachers diagnose where and why a pupil may not be successful in using each method. Again I am trying to help teachers focus on the pupil and what he brings to the maths problem.

1 Rounding up, e.g. 98 → 100 or 995 → 1000

For example where one number is near ten, hundred, thousand, etc. such as 758 + 196

> 196 is rounded up to 200 and added to 758 to give 958
>
> 4 is subtracted to re-adjust to the addition of 196
>
> giving an answer of 954.

What are the essential sub skills?

- ◆ An appreciation that you can adjust numbers to make them easier to use.
- ◆ A knowledge of the consequences for the intermediate answer of the adjustment, knowing if this intermediate answer is bigger or smaller than the final answer.
- ◆ Knowing how to make this adjustment.
- ◆ Knowing basic addition facts is less essential in this strategy, but can be used as a check. (In this example, knowing 8 + 6 = 14 checks the units digit).
- ◆ Remembering the question.

2 Balance and adjust

For example 86 − 38

> 86 is adjusted to 88 by adding 2
>
> 88 − 38 = 50
>
> adjust back by subtracting 2 to give 48.

What are the essential sub skills?

- ◆ An appreciation that you can adjust numbers to make them easier to use.
- ◆ A knowledge of the consequences for the intermediate answer of the adjustment, knowing if this intermediate answer is bigger or smaller than the final answer.

- Knowing how to make this adjustment.
- Knowing basic subtraction facts is less essential in this strategy, but can be used as a check. (In this example, knowing □6 − □8 = □8 checks the units digit.)
- Remembering the question.

3 Counting on

This is such an early skill, used for examples such as 9 − 5, but now involves appreciating how to bridge tens, hundreds, etc.

This method lends itself to modelling with coins (and was used in shops prior to computerised tills).

For example 86 − 38

Start with 38 and add to reach 40 (2)

Add tens to reach 80 (40)

Add to reach 86 (6)

Add up the answers from the three steps 2 + 40 + 6 = 48.

What are the essential sub skills?

- An appreciation that you can add instead of subtract.
- Knowing how to make this adjustment.
- Appreciating the significance of the place values of tens, hundreds, etc.
- Knowing how much to add each time, though this can be achieved by counting, but with the potential to affect short term memory load.
- Remembering the intermediate numbers added on and making the cumulative total.
- Remembering the question.

4 Working from left to right

For many pupils mental methods are merely written methods they do in their heads, so adding from left to right will not be a natural inclination.

For example, 374 + 567

Add 300 to 500 to give 800

Add 70 to 60 to give 130

Add 130 to 800 to give 930

Add 4 to 7 to give 11

Add 11 to 930 to give 941.

What are
the essential
sub skills?

◆   Knowing addition facts (but counting on is a possibility).
◆   Remembering the last addition each time.
◆   *Remembering the question.*

This method has two memory benefits. The answer is generated in the correct order of digits. The intermediate steps rehearse the intermediate answers.

5 Equal additions for subtraction

A method from my own school days.

For example 82 − 57

Although not essential the sum is usually pictured in the vertical form:

$$8^1 2$$
$$-\,^6\!\!5\ 7$$

Ten is added to the 2 to make 12 so the units subtraction becomes 12 − 7 (= 5)
    An equalising ten is added to the subtracting number so the 50 becomes 60 and the final answer is 25. (I confess that I never knew how this worked, but it did and I got the necessary ticks for my subtractions. I was particularly bemused by the fact that the tens digit of the subtracting number got bigger. I understand now and will use the method if under pressure to rush out an answer and feel secure about it being correct. Old habits die hard.)

What are
the essential
sub skills?

◆   A good visual memory.
◆   Adding in the tens in the correct places.
◆   Good recall of basic facts (counting on or back is going to push the short term memory further towards overload).
◆   Blind faith in the method!
◆   An ability to reverse the digits of the derived answer (done from units to hundreds) back into the correct hundreds, tens, units sequence.
◆   An ability to visualise the method in an organised and clear form.

6 Using the written algorithm mentally

The learner has to visualise the question as if it were written on paper and be able to hold that image and work on it as the computation progresses (see p.22).

What are
the essential
sub skills?

◆   A good visual memory.
◆   Good recall of basic facts (counting on or back is going to push the short term memory further towards overload).
◆   Recall of procedures for carrying or decomposing.

♦ An ability to reverse the digits of the derived answer (done from units to hundreds) back into the correct hundreds, tens, units sequence.

♦ Estimation skills for a crude check of the final answer. (Failure using this method is likely to be a long way from the correct answer.)

To sum up

There is almost always more than one way to solve a maths problem, however simple it seems to be. Children will become better problem solvers if they can think of 'another way' to solve a problem. This will also help them check their answers and become more confident with their answers. Adults can still learn this skill, though in the case of adults the skill is probably already there, it just needs drawing out. Learning to leave the old skill behind for a time while you learn another, almost contradictory skill, is hard for any sports player. It's hard to do in academic activities, too. The old safe secure methods are just that, safe and secure. They may be inefficient, but the early stages of learning the new skill may appear even less efficient. Hopefully that will change and the new skill can take its place alongside the old skill.

The grasshopper style involves the key skill of overviewing and estimating and the inchworm style involves the key skill of seeing the details and documenting procedures. Encouraging flexibility in thinking style is yet another aspect of the risk taking classroom ethos needed to develop successful, non-anxious mathematicians.

Remember, there may be some inchworms and some grasshoppers whose thinking style is terminal and totally impervious to change, however skilled the teacher!

Chapter 5

Developmental perspectives

Much of maths is developmental. Some psychologists write about a hierarchy of cognitive development, but some aspects of development are more simple than that and others are more sophisticated. Whenever a teacher or tutor is working on a maths topic the question 'What else are you teaching?' is very relevant. It may be that a concept is being introduced or that a previously recognised pattern is being revisited in a new form. Each topic is likely to be setting the groundwork for future topics, so there is a need to know where the maths is going when taking the first steps on that mathematical journey.

At a later the stage the question may well change to be 'Where did this problem begin?' If a learner's grasp on mathematics is not robust his learning may break down when faced by a more challenging development.

The 'simple' aspect of development concerns basic skills and knowledge. For example, not knowing that $6 \times 7 = 42$ would handicap a pupil working on the problem 26×17. If the marking of this sum is based purely on right/wrong, then a wrong answer is a wrong answer and does not judge that the method has been mastered and lack of knowledge of one fact was the error. The pupil cannot develop skills in long multiplication without support for his deficit, which is, in this example, recall of basic multiplication facts.

A more complex situation illustrates the multi-faceted aspects of progression. Faced with a question such as $635 - 197$ an inchworm and a grasshopper (Chapter 4) will use quite different procedures to obtain their answers. Each will be drawing on different supporting skills and using different concepts. Let's assume that both the inchworm pupil and the grasshopper pupil are skilled.

The inchworm pupil will need a good visual memory to 'see' the sum in his mind as

$$
\begin{array}{r}
635 \\
-197 \\
\hline
\end{array}
$$

He will then subtract starting at units moving through to hundreds, decomposing merrily and then reversing the order of the digits from his workings to give an answer of 438. Conceptually he has understood (or at least remembered) the procedure and he has the abilities to carry out the process. He may or may not understand decomposition (in its mathematical sense).

The grasshopper pupil will consider the values of the individual numbers and their relative values. He will perceive the 197 as very close to 200 and have a first estimate of the answer as over 400, probably estimating at a little more than 435. He adjusts for the approximate subtraction of 200 by adding back 3 to obtain 438. His conceptual understanding has focused less on procedure and more on the relative values of numbers. So, the grasshopper has appreciated the order and size of number by rounding 197 up to 200. He has also understood that the subtraction of 200 gave a smaller answer (compared to subtracting 197) and adjusted by adding 3. His conceptual understanding has focused on the values of numbers.

I think it would be a difficult argument to decide which method was higher up the cognitive development ladder. And that's with taking as an example a relatively straightforward whole number subtraction problem. Analysing the way a task can be approached is a fascinating activity. All the cognitive factors which are involved in a mathematics task can be a source of the problem, so it may be just one factor that is the cause or it could be the interaction of several factors and then may well include anxiety, attitude and other factors from the affective domain.

If we understand some of the development of mathematical ideas we are better able to diagnose where difficulties lie for then we can track back until we find the root of the problem. For example, for the development of multiplication skills and concepts a sequence could be:

$7 \times 6,$

$12 \times 8,$

$34 \times 45,$

$s + s + s + s = 4s,$

$q + q + q + r + r = 3q + 2r,$

$5y + 2y = 7y,$

$4y + 3w + 3y + 2w = 7y + 5w,$

$a(x + y) = ax + ay,$

$(a + x)(b + y) = ab + ay + bx + xy$

with $6 \times \frac{1}{3}, \frac{1}{2} \times \frac{3}{4}$ somewhere in the later stages of the sequence.

It can be valuable to consider a sequence backwards as well as forwards. Some may not see 7×6 as a true member of the sequence, but if your strategy to access 7×6 is 5×6 plus 2×6 then it is very much the first member of the sequence. The common themes in the sequence are multiplication as repeated addition and partial products.

7×6 is $6 + 6 + 6 + 6 + 6 + 6 + 6$ which is grouped as
$6 + 6 + 6 + 6 + 6 (5 \times 6)$ and $6 + 6 (2 \times 6)$

12×8 can be seen as 10×8 plus 2×8,
based on $8 + 8 + 8 + 8 + 8 + 8 + 8 + 8 + 8 + 8 + 8 + 8$

34×45 is often computed from two partial products 30×45 and 4×45

$s + s + s + s$ is algebra for, for example $7 + 7 + 7 + 7$,
giving $4s$ and its equivalent 4×7

$q + q + q + r + r$ becomes $3q + 2r$

$5y + 2y$ is the algebra version of $5 \times 6 + 2 \times 6$ and becomes $7y$

$4y + 3w + 3y + 2w$ groups like terms as $7y + 5w$

$a(x + y)$ requires that both x and y are multiplied by a to give $ax + ay$
which is another algebra version of 7×6 as $6(5 + 2)$ and also a reminder
of the commutative property, that is $7 \times 6 = 6 \times 7$

$(a + x)(b + y)$ is the algebra version of 34×45 as $(30 + 4)(40 + 5)$
and the understanding of this could well have begun at 7×6, linking
multiplication and addition and grouping additions to make partial
products.

(All the above examples can have an associated simple area diagram to emphasise the common theme, for example Figure 5.1.)

In the 'Framework for the National Numeracy Strategy: Reception to Year 6'
there are two pages assigned to 'Laying the foundations for algebra' addressing
the contribution of skills such as

$3 + \square = 10$

and the need to understand the commutative, associative and distributive laws.

Times table facts

Some people find learning and recalling these 121 facts a virtually impossible task.
If they persevere in trying to rote learn them then anxiety increases while self
confidence decreases. The times table facts are important facts which make a very
large contribution to numeracy. If it is possible to learn them then they should be
learned. Their use pervades maths curricula as is illustrated below for the single
fact $3 \times 7 = 21$:

$3 \times 7 = 21$

3×17

38×47

30×70

300×700

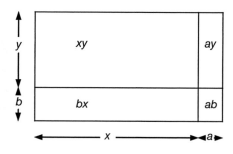

$$(x + a)(y + b) = xy + bx + ay + ab$$

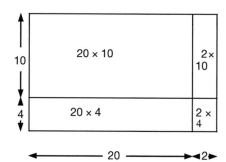

$$22 \times 14 = 20 \times 10 + 20 \times 4 + 2 \times 10 + 2 \times 4$$

$$22 \times 14 = \quad 200 \quad + \quad 80 \quad + \quad 20 \quad + \quad 8$$

$$= \quad 308$$

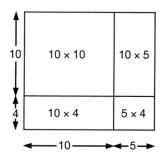

$$15 \times 14 = 10 \times 10 + 10 \times 5 + 10 \times 4 + 5 \times 4$$

$$15 \times 14 = \quad 100 \quad + \quad 50 \quad + \quad 40 \quad + \quad 20$$

$$= \quad 210$$

(see also as 10×14 plus $\frac{1}{2} \times 10 \times 14$)

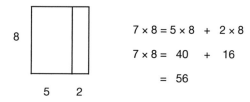

$$7 \times 8 = 5 \times 8 \ + \ 2 \times 8$$

$$7 \times 8 = \quad 40 \quad + \quad 16$$

$$= \quad 56$$

Figure 5.1 Area models for multiplication

and for division:

$$3\overline{)6210}$$

and for multiplication and division in two steps:

$$45 \times 21 = 45 \times 3 \times 7$$

$$756 \div 21 = 756 \div 3 = 252 \div 7 = 36$$

and for fractions:

$$\frac{2}{3} + \frac{1}{7} = \frac{14}{21} + \frac{3}{21} = \frac{17}{21}$$

and decimals:

$$0.3 \times 0.7 = 0.21$$

$$0.03 \times 0.07 = 0.0021$$

and percentages:

$$30\% \text{ of } 70 = \frac{30}{100} \times 70 = 21$$

and money:

$$3 \times 7p = 21p$$

$$3 \times £7 = £21$$

and measures:

$$3 \times 7\,g = 3 \times \frac{7}{1000}\,kg = 0.021\,kg$$

and negative numbers:

$$-3 \times -7 = +21$$

and shape and space:

$$\text{Area} = 1 \times b = 3\,m \times 7\,m = 21\,m^2$$

and algebra:

$$a + a + a = 3a$$

$$b + b + b + b + b + b + b = 7b$$

$$3a \times 7b = 21ab$$

$$x^2 + 4x - 21 = (x + 7)(x - 3) \quad x^2 + 10x + 21 = (x + 7)(x + 3)$$

and word problems:

Mike buys three pens at 7p each.

How many days in three weeks?

How to teach times table facts to students who cannot rote learn them

The following suggestions use developmental methods which are based on the grasshopper skill of breaking down and building up numbers. The strategies are sufficiently consistent for most inchworms to adapt to them and they can only increase awareness of flexible ways to learn maths.

The principles

✔ Use the easy facts (1×, 2×, 5×, 10×) to work out the harder facts, that is, build on what is known;

✔ use two easy steps when one step is too hard;

✔ and there are only 21 harder facts.

First put the problem into perspective. Learning, or more accurately forgetting these facts is an issue. Newspapers love it: 'Back to basics . . . everyone will learn their tables' (and presumably move onwards and upwards thereafter). Adults with selective memories say 'We all learned them. We sat and chanted them till we did.' All this mythical nonsense piles on the pressure for those who don't achieve success in this particular task. A teacher may well have the double task of teaching the multiplication facts and restoring the learner's self-esteem so that he believes that he can succeed. So let's put the numbers into perspective . . .

A table square for the 0× to 10× facts has 121 facts for multiplication (and 121 for division). A blank square (Figure 5.2) looks daunting, but if the facts for 0, 1, 2, 5 and 10 are filled in then there are only 36 facts left (Figure 5.3). Six of these are the squares (3^2, 4^2, 6^2, 7^2, 8^2, 9^2). The remaining 30 may be halved to fifteen due to the commutative property of $ab = ba$. So there are 21 remaining facts beyond the 'easy' ones.

	0	1	2	3	4	5	6	7	8	9	10
0											
1											
2											
3											
4											
5											
6											
7											
8											
9											
10											

Figure 5.2 The blank table square

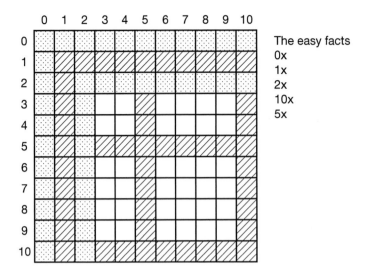

Figure 5.3 The almost complete table square, with the 'easy' number facts shaded

(For full details of the methods described below and mature graphics try the CD-ROM 'What to do when you can't Learn the Times Tables', Appendix 1.)

What is left may be derived from the easy facts:

- 9× derived from 10× using a predictable pattern (which also teaches estimation and adjustment).
- 4× derived by doubling the 2× facts (teaching cumulative multiplication, such as 30× as 3× followed by 10×).
- 3× derived by partial products 2× plus 1× (teaching partial products and thus 'long' multiplication).
- 6× derived by partial products 5× plus 1×.
- 7× derived by partial products 5× plus 2×.
- 8× actually only 8 × 8 is left, so just keep doubling till you reach 64! (or more sensibly use 8 as 2^3)

9×

The pattern is that $9n = 10n - n$ which can be demonstrated with Cuisenaire rods (9 and 10) arranged as area, for example see Figure 5.4.

Six lots of nine are six less than six lots of ten.

$$6 \times 9 = 60 - 6 = 54 \text{ (and to check, add the digits } 5 + 4 = 9)$$

Twenty-three lots of nine are twenty-three lots of ten minus twenty three.

$$23 \times 9 = 230 - 23 = 207 \text{ (and to check add the digits } 2 + 0 + 7 = 9)$$

The digits of the answer will always add to 9 (useful as a check and for division to know if nine is a factor).

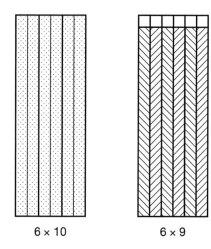

Comparing the two areas ...

$6 \times 9 = 6 \times 10 - 6 \times 1$

$(9n = 10n - n)$

6 × 10   6 × 9

Figure 5.4 6 × 10 compared to 6 × 9

This procedure also teaches estimation and how to refine an estimation. For the refinement, the question, 'Is the answer bigger or smaller?' is once again apposite.

4×

Simply double twice, for example:

4×7 start with $2 \times 7 = 14$

then double again $2 \times 14 = 28$

As with the ten strategy for 9, the double double strategy for 4 works with numbers beyond the table square collection.

The developmental uses of this property are illustrated below, starting with the algebraic generalisation, illustrating again the 'What else are you teaching?' facet of this approach.

If $y = ab$ then $xy = x \times a \times b = xab$

For example,

4×6	$2 \times 6 = 12$	$12 \times 2 = 24$
34×6	$34 \times 3 = 102$	$102 \times 2 = 204$
31×20	$31 \times 2 = 62$	$62 \times 10 = 620$
67×300	$67 \times 3 = 201$	$201 \times 100 = 20100$
71×0.2	$71 \times 2 = 142$	$142 \times \frac{1}{10} = 14.2$
$248 \div 4$	$248 \div 2 = 124$	$124 \div 2 = 62$ (and $\div 8$ just takes one more step)

$2 \times 15 = 30$ $15 = 5 \times 3$ $30 = 2 \times 3 \times 5$

$248 \times \frac{1}{8}$ $248 \times \frac{1}{2} = 124$ $124 \times \frac{1}{2} = 62$ $62 \times \frac{1}{2} = 31$

$84 \times \frac{2}{3}$ $84 \times \frac{1}{3} = 28$ $28 \times 2 = 56$

The use of two steps is sometimes not needed, but sometimes unavoidable for mathematical mortals.

3×, 6× and 7×

Use partial products (see Figure 5.5).

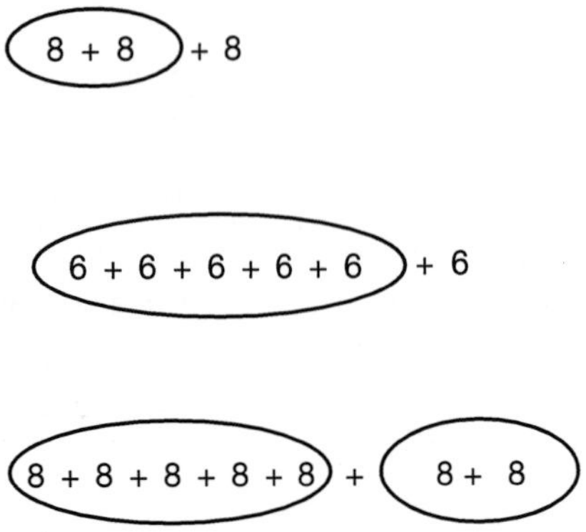

(8 + 8) + 8

(6 + 6 + 6 + 6 + 6) + 6

(8 + 8 + 8 + 8 + 8) + (8 + 8)

Figure 5.5 Grouping repeated additions into partial products

so $3 \times 8 = 2 \times 8$ plus $1 \times 8 = 16 + 8 = 24$

and $6 \times 6 = 5 \times 6$ plus $1 \times 6 = 30 + 6 = 36$

and $7 \times 8 = 5 \times 8$ plus $2 \times 8 = 40 + 16 = 56$ (and did you know that $56 = 7 \times 8$ has 5678 in order?)

This strategy has introduced the procedure for 'long' multiplications, for example 23×51 becomes 20×51 plus $3 \times 51 = 1020 + 153 = 1173$.

This, the distributive law, can be generalised via algebra and some of its developmental aspects summarised as

If $y = a + b$ then $xy = x(a + b) = ax + bx$

For example,

$3 \times 5 = 5(2 + 1) = 5 \times 2 + 5 \times 1 = 10 + 5$

$6 \times 8 = 8(5 + 1) = 5 \times 8 + 1 \times 8 = 40 + 8$

$12 \times 13 = 13(10 + 2) = 10 \times 13 + 2 \times 13 = 130 + 26 = 156$

$17 \times 9 = 17(10 - 1) = 17 \times 10 - 17 \times 1 = 170 - 17 = 153$

$42 \times 99 = 42(100 - 1) = 4200 - 42 = 4158$

$15\% \text{ of } 440 = (10\% + 5\%) \text{ of } 440 \qquad 44 + 22 = 66$

$75\% \text{ of } 440 = (50\% + 25\%) \text{ of } 440 \qquad 220 + 110 = 330$

$52 \times 81 = 81(50 + 2) = 81 \times 50 + 81 \times 2 = 4050 + 162 = 4212$

$\frac{3}{4} \times 40 = 40(\frac{1}{2} + \frac{1}{4}) = 20 + 10 = 30$

$0.55 \times 68 = 68(0.5 + 0.05) = 34 + 3.4 = 37.4$

The area model

Just a reminder that these multiplications can be shown by an area model. Figure 5.1, page 79.

Multiplication facts later in the curriculum (or life)

Multiplication facts are just a set of facts which are stored in the memory. If they are accessed by strategies such as those described in this chapter then the recall of a multiplication fact may also be a skill, which also has to be remembered. If a fact is not used regularly then it will be less prominent in the memory. If a skill is not practised regularly then it will be less efficient.

So it could be that a lot of time is invested by learner and teacher in accessing these facts and that two or three years later, the need for these facts is less perhaps because a calculator is used, or perhaps because 8×7 and its friends are less a part of the mathematics curriculum. So it should not be a surprise to either the learner or the teacher if the recall and the skill have declined in speed or accuracy or both.

This note of caution applies, obviously, to many other areas of mathematics and is a most important reason to use a spiral structure for the mathematics curriculum, and a spiral with a small pitch to ensure frequent returns to all topics.

Multiplication facts and examinations

Examinations always put extra pressure on insecure learners. For many such learners extra time may be granted for the examination. One use of extra time is to write down key information at the start of the examination before anxiety kicks in at full intensity. Learners can be shown how to draw up a tables square quite quickly and efficiently, drawing on the linking strategies described above. It will be a great help if they are allowed to take squared paper into the examination, then all they have to do is fill in the 'easy' facts, $0\times$, $1\times$, $2\times$, $10\times$, $5\times$ (checking back to $10\times$ and the odd/even pattern), $4\times$ from $2\times$, $9\times$ from $10\times$, $3\times$ by adding $2\times$ and $1\times$ and there are then only nine spaces left which can be filled in as and when required, again using the linking strategies (and maybe the 5678 sequence for $7 \times 8 = 56$ which clears away another two gaps). This use of easy facts and easy strategies leaves only 5 distinct facts.

Long multiplication using 'easy numbers' partial products

e.g.   677 × 73

1 Find the easy numbers in 73

73 = 50 + 20 + 2 + 1

2 Set up an easy numbers multiples table

677 × 1 =   677

677 × 2 =   1354   (do as 1200 + 140 + 14)

677 × 5 =   3385   (do as 677 × 10 ÷ 2)

677 × 10 = 6770

677 × 20 = 13540

677 × 50 = 33850   (look for the ×10, ×100
etc. patterns)

3 Add up the partial products

677 × 73

677 × **50** =   33850
677 × **20** =   13540
677 × **2** =   1354
677 × **1** =   677

677 × **73** =   <u>49421</u>

Long division using 'easy numbers' partial products

e.g.   3416 ÷ 56

1 Set up the easy numbers multiples table

56 × 1 =   56

56 × 2 =   112

56 × 5 =   280

56 × 10 =   560

56 × 20 = 1120

56 × 50 = 2800

56 × 100 = 5600   (look for the ×10, ×100
etc. patterns)

2 Look at the multiples which result in answers near 3416

The answer lies between 50 and 100, probably closer to 50 than 100

3. Add multiples until the target (3416) is reached

2800	50
560	10
3360	60

3360	60
56	1
3416	<u>61</u>

The division could also be done by subtracting the easy number multiples from 3416

Figure 5.6 Multiplication and division using the 'easy' numbers

The easy multiplication facts, long multiplication and long division

Traditional long multiplication is multiplication using partial products. For example, 782 × 43 would be done as 782 × 40 plus 782 × 3. Similarly traditional long division is done by subtraction of partial products, for example 6919 ÷ 37 will start with a subtraction of 3700 (37 × 100) then subtraction of 2960 (37 × 80) and finally 259 (37 × 7), to give an answer of 187. In both these examples the learner has no choice of partial product. The method dictates which ones to use. In the division example, these are 100×, 80× and 7×. This may be a problem if the learner has weak and possibly inaccurate recall of 8× and 7× facts.

Alternative structuring of multiplication and division by partial products using the 'easy' numbers is shown in Figure 5.6 opposite. These methods relate multiplication to repeated addition and division to repeated addition and subtraction.

Number bonds for 10

$$10 \quad 9 \quad 8 \quad 7 \quad 6 \quad 5 \quad 4 \quad 3 \quad 2 \quad 1 \quad 0$$

$$0 \quad 1 \quad 2 \quad 3 \quad 4 \quad 5 \quad 6 \quad 7 \quad 8 \quad 9 \quad 10$$

These are truly key facts. They can be presented in a range of images, from rods to fingers to coins (Figure 5.7) but if they can be learned they will pay back the effort used many times. At exam times, when anxious pupils may forget even their most carefully remembered facts, it takes only a moment to recreate the figure above. Note that the anchor fact 5 + 5 is emphasised and used as a check.

Simple card games can be used to practise these facts, such as pelmanism. The facts should be remembered as addition facts, for example 6 + 4 = 10, but also as missing addends, for example, 6 + □ = 10, which is one of the foundations for algebra and also leads to the subtraction fact, 10 − 6 = 4.

Extensions and development of the number bonds for 10

These eleven facts can be developed into many more facts. By anchoring any new facts back to the number bonds for ten, the learner has a check and once again, number facts are being inter-related.

Number bonds for 9 and 11

◆ The number bonds for 9 use the relationship that 9 is 1 less than 10. Thus, for example 5 + 5 = 10 is adjusted to 5 + 4 = 9 and 4 + 5 = 9.

◆ The number bonds for 11 use the relationship that 11 is 1 more than 10. Thus, for example 5 + 5 = 10 is adjusted to 5 + 6 = 11 and 6 + 5 = 11.

◆ Even in this simple exercise the language 'less than' and 'more than' is revised. Relating 11 and 9 to 10 is reinforcing estimation skills and acknowledging that 9 is both 5 + 4 and 4 + 5 revises the commutative property of numbers.

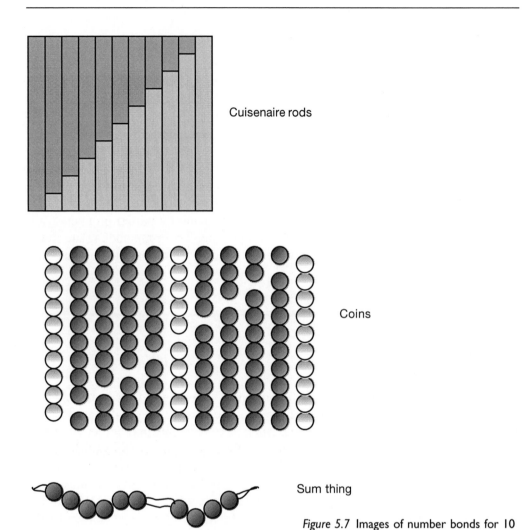

Cuisenaire rods

Coins

Sum thing

Figure 5.7 Images of number bonds for 10

Number bonds for 100, 1000, 10,000 and 1

This introduces a simple extension of the pattern in terms of 100, 1000 and upwards. The (decimal) number bonds for 1 may be a greater step for some children. In each extension the use of visual images may help, though, as ever, these may have to be the personal choice of the individual learner (see Figure 5.8).

The extension from 7 + 3 to 70 + 30 is fairly straightforward. The extension to 75 + 25 requires a revisit to 10 as 9 + 1.

The extension to 0.3 + 0.7 could be modelled with 10p coins, after establishing that 10p is 0.1 of £1 and 20p is 0.2 of £1 (calculators 'remove' the end 0 from 0.10 and 0.20 to make them 0.1 and 0.2).

Estimation

The understanding of 10 and its neighbouring numbers helps set the foundations for estimation skills. So, knowing that 9 is close to 10, 8 is close but less close than 9, 11 is close, 12 is close but less close than 11 can be extended to numbers around 90, 900, 0.9, 0.09, and so on. Visual images could be base ten materials

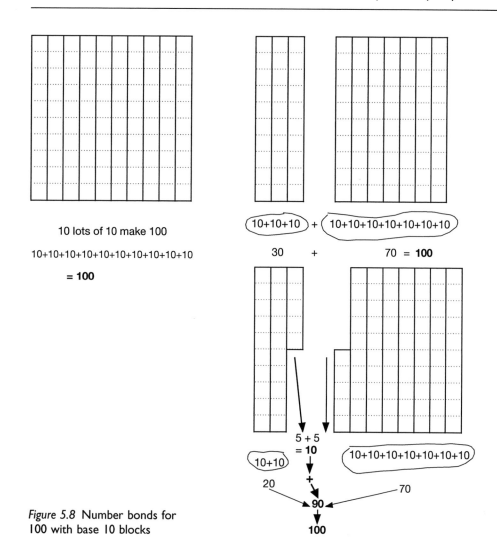

10 lots of 10 make 100

10+10+10+10+10+10+10+10+10+10

= 100

$\boxed{10+10+10}$ + $\boxed{10+10+10+10+10+10+10}$

30 + 70 = **100**

5 + 5
= **10**

$\boxed{10+10}$ $\boxed{10+10+10+10+10+10+10}$

20 + 70

90

100

Figure 5.8 Number bonds for 100 with base 10 blocks

and money, with money more abstract as in asking what is the nearest whole pound value to £13.99? Money, of course, takes us into everyday maths.

Adding by casting out 10s

A column of numbers can be added by casting out combinations which make 10. For example

^{3}34
9~~2~~
3~~3~~
8~~1~~   1 + 9 = 10
7~~5~~
48   casting out the 2, 3, 5, 1 and 9 leaves only 8 + 4, which could
+5~~9~~   be quickly counted on. Three (10s) are 'carried' over to the
‾‾‾‾   tens column
422

2 + 3 + 5 = 10

The procedure can be repeated for the tens column, casting out $8 + 7 + 5 = 20$, $3 + 3 + 4 = 10$, leaving $9 + 3 = 12$. Adding up these tens gives 42 tens, that is 420.

To work out an average (mean) learners have to add a group of numbers. This method may enable them to do that accurately, so that the addition sub-skill of working out an average is circumvented.

Subtraction

Number bonds for 10 and 100 are especially useful once again when subtracting by counting on through tens, hundreds and thousands.

It is also useful to remember the number bonds in 'subtraction' format, for example as with

$$4 + \square = 10$$

Remember: revision of basic facts can be done in many topic settings, for example with angles. Number sums for 90° and 180° allow learners to practise addition and subtraction skills in a new context.

The addition square

Using the same principle as for the multiplication facts, the addition facts square can be used to demonstrate progress through the task and the impact of learning key facts and inter-relating them to new facts. Once again the starting challenge is 121 facts, which reduces as easy facts and links are mastered.

Facts	Number of facts left to learn
	121
adding on zero 0	100
adding on 1 and 2 (finger counting)	64
adding on 10 (place value pattern)	49
adding on 9 (add on 10, subtract 1)	36
number bonds for 10	31
number bonds for 10 ± 1	21
doubles	16
doubles ± 1	10

5 + 3	3 + 5	(which relates to 4 + 4)
7 + 5	5 + 7	(which relates to 6 + 6)
8 + 4	4 + 8	
8 + 5	5 + 8	
8 + 6	6 + 8	(which relates to 7 + 7)

Levels of learning

Returning to the introductory paragraph of this chapter and the psychological inter-pretation of developmental mathematics, a number of psychologists from Piaget to Gagne have looked at levels or hierarchies of learning. This complements the discussions above on the developmental nature of mathematics, which has considered development from a maths content perspective. Gagne described four levels of learning.[1]

Associative (rote) learning

Associative learning is establishing a memorised response to the presentation of a stimulus. It focuses on memorisation and mastery. For example, pupils learn the six times table and can respond '42' automatically when asked 'What is 7×6 ?' or a teacher demonstrates 'decomposition' and pupils then practise ten examples of decomposing.

Concept learning

Concept learning occurs when children attempt to identify characteristics that determine inclusion in or exclusion from a set or class. It focuses on categorising, classifying, ordering and labelling. For example, children learn that $\frac{1}{2}$, $\frac{4}{5}$, $\frac{71}{99}$, $\frac{5}{3}$ can all be classified as 'fractions' or pupils know that both the drawings below contain *three* items

Principle learning

Principle learning occurs when children attempt to relate ideas. For example, pupils use the distributive property ($7 \times 5 = 5 \times 5 + 2 \times 5$) in new situations such as:

$$5 \times 34 = 5 \times 30 + 5 \times 4$$

Problem solving

Problem solving occurs when children employ principles to achieve a goal. It focuses on applying, verifying and proving. Pupils must both select and apply certain principles in order to arrive at a solution. They integrate skills, concepts and principles into a cognitive structure. For example, in solving a word problem such as:

Mike and Sam decide to share a Coke and a packet of crisps. Cokes cost 45p and crisps cost 35p. How much does each boy pay?

To sum up

Mathematics is a very developmental subject. Facts develop, procedures develop and concepts develop. The foundations are set with the early experiences. Concepts start to build with these early experiences and equally misconceptions may start to build in these early times, too. So, from a pre-emptive perspective, it is important to minimise the misconceptions by being aware of where they may occur and where the current work will lead mathematically. From the intervention perspective it is important to be able to look back and be aware of where the foundations for the current work were set, where the gaps are and the implications of those 'holes' for the learner.

So taking a developmental perspective means being able to look forwards and backwards at the learner and each 'new' maths topic.

Chapter 6

The language of maths

I've given a separate, albeit short chapter to this topic because it causes so many children difficulty.

In the early stages difficulties are largely a consequence of the peculiarities and irregularities of many maths words in the English language, for example the use of the same words and phrases in everyday life as well as for maths can be a source of confusion. Later it is a consequence of the way word problems are written and constructed. So the problems and confusions are both with the vocabulary of maths and with the language (semantics) of maths.

As an example of problems with the vocabulary in the early stages of maths, consider the next nine two digit numbers after 10. They start with eleven and twelve which are exceptions, one-off words, then they take the digit order and reverse it as in 13 as thirteen, then fourteen, fifteen, sixteen, seventeen, eighteen and nineteen. Thirteen and fifteen compound the eccentricity of the teen numbers by not being threeteen and fiveteen, and of course all of them end in teen rather than ten. The twenties and beyond then fall into a pattern where the words tally with the digit order, although thirty, forty, fifty, sixty, seventy, eighty and ninety as words are irregular in the sense that they are not three ten, (threety would be a step in the consistent direction) four ten and so on as happens with one hundred, two hundred, three hundred and so on.

As an example of a language comprehension difficulty we have word problems such as, 'Mark has two more toys than James. Mark has ten toys. How many toys does James have?' The key vocabulary which normally hints at the operation '+' is 'more', one of several words we can use to infer addition, but here the question requires a subtraction, 10 − 2. So, having taught the child that the vocabulary for + can be said as 'add, more, plus, and' he then meets 'more' used in the language of a maths question where the interpretation has to be 'subtract'.

So, the main difficulties and confusions in the words of maths come from aspects involving vocabulary and then in the interpretation and comprehension of the language used to write mathematics word problems.

The teen numbers (and eleven and twelve)

As mentioned above, the teen numbers are probably the first inconsistency in the language of maths that children meet. The numbers from 11 to 19 do not have names which fit the pattern of later numbers. For example, compare thirteen with twenty-three, thirty-three, forty-three and so on to ninety-three. Thirteen is said as unit-ten, 23, 33 and so on are said as ten-unit, that is in the same sequence as the digits. Whilst we often take pains to encourage children to look for the pattern, we should warn them of this particular exception. Basically they have to learn the first nineteen numbers as exceptions to the rule before they can start to look for a pattern. Fortunately most children simply absorb the information by repetition. The teen numbers occur frequently in everyday life.

One of the, not surprising, consequences of the order of the components of teen words is that pupils may transpose numbers. For example they may write 51 for fifteen. It may help to use manipulatives such as base ten blocks or coins to re-inforce the correct order of digits or arrow cards (Figure 6.1) or claim that the teen numbers are as difficult as teenagers.

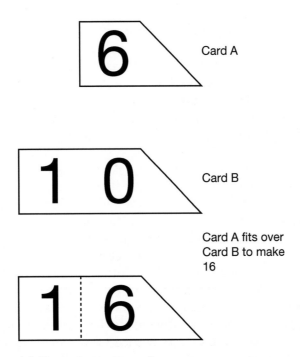

Card A

Card B

Card A fits over
Card B to make
16

Figure 6.1 Place value arrow cards

The 'dual' vocabulary of maths

The vocabulary of mathematics is full of examples of inconsistencies, and as has been said before, insecure learners do not like or cope well with inconsistencies. The colloquial nature of some maths vocabulary, that is words used in mathematics which are used with different meanings in everyday non-mathematical language, is a good example of pupils having to adjust to inconsistencies, in this case in the meaning of a familiar word. Note the interchanging use of the words maths and mathematics (and sometimes arithmetic).

Children have to learn that some words and phrases they have been using in everyday language have a specific meaning when used in a maths context, for example, from the National Numeracy Strategy, in Reception, 'sort, match and count' and in Year 5, 'operation and capacity'. Most of the examples below are taken from the English National Numeracy Strategy.

acute (angle)	acute (pain)
altogether	the Emperor's New Clothes à la Danny Kaye
angle	what's your angle?
anti	auntie
ascending/descending order	could be a literal interpretation writing numbers downwards
behind the chair	behind with my work (left) behind behind (buttocks)
borrow (in subtraction)	borrow (lend)
bracket ( )	bracket (for shelf)
by as in 6m by 8m	by the river 'bye bye'
cancel (fraction)	cancel (ticket)
capacity (volume)	capacity (potential)
carry (addition)	carry (a bag)
chord (circle)	chord (music)
clockwise	streetwise
compass (circle)	compass (NESW)
count $(1, 2, 3 \ldots)$	Count Dracula
count on (in numbers)	count on (me)
degree (°)	degree (BSc)
difference between two numbers $(-)$	difference in appearance
digit (3)	digit (finger)
divide $(\div)$	divide and rule the path divides
double $(\times 2)$	'you must have a double'
even numbers	the odds are even even him!
expand (brackets)	expand (balloon)
expression $(xy + 3)$	expression (on a face)
face (on a shape)	your face
factor $(15 = 5 \times 3)$	factor 5 sun screen
formula $(d = st)$	Formula One
function $(f\{x\})$	function (room)
goes into	enters

half ($\frac{1}{2}$) with 'half' as a precise concept	half a pizza with 'half' as an estimate
heavy (weight)	heavy metal
horizontal and vertical	which means what?
hour	our
index (x^3)	index (book)
interval (data)	interval (theatre)
key (calculator)	key (symbol)
	key (idea)
	key (lock)
	quay
left (right)	left behind
light (weight)	light (bulb)
long (length)	long (time)
makes (equals)	makes (a cake)
mass (in kg)	mass (in church)
match (compare)	match (strike a)
mean (average)	mean (nasty)
mixed number	aren't most numbers mixed?
multiple of 5	multiple injuries
negative (-7)	negative (critical)
net (flat pack)	net (fishing)
odd numbers	odd person
	odd you should say that
operation ($+$, $-$, $\times$, $\div$)	operation (hospital)
order	last orders
	religious order
	obey orders
place value	value of a place (in the sun)
plane	plane (747)
	plane (wood)
	plain
pi	pie
pound (£)	(dog) pound
pound (lb)	pound (pummel)
power	(world) power
	power (strength)
prime (number)	prime (location)
prism	prison
product ($6 \times 7 = 42$)	product (manufactured)
proper/improper	yes

range	Range (Rover)
	range (shooting)
reduced to . . .	reduced to tears
reflex (angle)	reflex (doctor and rubber hammer)
relationship between numbers	relationship between people
remainder	remainders (bargains)
remove (the brackets)	remove (literally)
	remove (take away, but not subtract)
right angle	wrong angle
roughly (close)	roughly (playing)
round (up or down)	round the garden
	round the block
	round (circular)
rule (metre)	rule (obey)
scale (1:10)	scale (weighing)
60 seconds	second place
share ($\div$)	Cher (!)
	share (stock exchange)
show your working	show you're working
sign (as in $\div$)	sign (road)
simplify (algebra and fractions)	simplify (make easier)
solution (solve)	solution (dissolve)
solve (the equation)	solve (the murder mystery)
sort (arrange)	sort (you out!)
substitute (in algebra)	substitute (soccer)
sum	some
table (data)	table (and chairs)
take away (subtract)	take away (food)
tall (height)	tall (story)
term (*ax*)	term (school)
thick line	thick glue
	thick
third ($\frac{1}{3}$)	third (3rd)
times	*Sunday Times*
	old times
	good times
total	total darkness
translation	translation (language)
Triangular number (value)	triangular number (shape 4)
units (tens, hundreds)	industrial units
week	weak
weight	wait

So, do not assume that the learner will automatically adjust to the new, maths meaning. They may be distracted by their original understanding of the word. They may be misled and diverted from the idea you are trying to purvey.

The four operations

Further inconsistencies arise with the basic operations, +, −, × and ÷. Even the word 'operation' is more usually associated with hospitals than with maths lessons. Perhaps because adding, subtracting, multiplying and, to a lesser extent, dividing are 'everyday' maths operations, they have attracted a varied vocabulary. So we can infer + by 'plus, add, more, increase, sum, total, and'. The learner has to cope with a choice of several words for the same maths operation. Some pupils, especially those with special needs, like consistency, so if they have internalised 'plus' as their word for +, then they may not accept 'and'.

These words have a second problem associated with them. As outlined above, they are not exclusive to maths and may have more than one meaning in maths, for example 'plus' can mean 'positive' or a bonus as in 'That's a plus.' This particular example is also clouded by the use of −8 to mean 'minus or negative 8' while we do not write the + sign for 'positive or plus' 8 when using integers.

These are well recognised confusions. For example Anne Henderson and Elaine Miles have both examined this language aspect of maths, but the flexibility of vocabulary can be something to celebrate, too, and pupils could be asked 'Can you think of another word we can use for this?'

Decimals

This is a similarity problem for some learners. The learner needs good auditory discrimination to hear the difference between ten and tenth, hundred and hundredth, thousand and thousandth. The sounds are similar, but the numbers they label are very different. This could be the one time that the 'slower and louder' intervention technique actually might be appropriate!

Little words, especially 'not'

Some of the learners who have weaker reading skills miss the little words when reading, such as 'and' or 'not'. Missing 'not' is a drastic error! It may help to use a highlighter pen for the little words, so that they are less likely to be overlooked.

Homophones

Another source of potential confusion and ineffective communication are homophones: words that sound the same as another, different word. For example, in this mental arithmetic problem

Aziz ate four of his eight apples. How many were left?

are 'ate' and 'eight' and 'four', which could be for as in 'Aziz ate for England!'.

Other homophones include:

one	won	
two	to	too
by	buy	
complementary	complimentary	
key	quay	
plane	plain	
prism	prison	
sine	sign	
sum	some	
weight	wait	

Writing word problems

Pupils usually meet word problems where they have to translate words to symbol sentences or equations. It is very useful for them to practise the opposite translation, that is symbols to words so that they can learn how a word problem can be composed.

So, for example, they could be asked to create a word problem for 8 − 3. The key words for subtract are less, left, minus, take away, subtract, difference.[1] A very basic statement would be,

'What is 8 minus 3?'

This can be re-worded to,

'What is 3 less than 8?' or

'What is left if I take 3 from 8?' or

'Take 3 away from 8' or

'Subtract 3 from 8' or

'8 take away 3' or

'What is the difference between 8 and 3?' (Often misinterpreted.)

But then children can be encouraged to add in more vocabulary and language variables

♦ Basic   What is 8 minus 3?

♦ Wrong order   Take 3 away from 8. (This can create
  (non-mathematical)   difficulty for insecure learners.)

◆ Wrong order (mathematical)	Subtract 3 from 8.
◆ Objects	Sam has 8 *toys*. Mike borrows 3 *toy*s from Sam. How many *toys* does Sam have left?
◆ Big words	*Samantha* has 8 *chocolate digestive biscuits.* She eats 3. How many are left?
◆ Two key words	Jay has lost some coins and has 8 *left*. He loses 3 *more*. How many coins does he have now?
◆ Superfluous data	Kev has 8 coins. *Mike has 6 coins.* Kev loses 3 coins. How many has he left?
◆ Words for numbers	Tia has *eight* cans of cola. She drinks *three*. How many has she left?
◆ No familiar key word	Jon juggles 8 balls. He drops 3. How many is he juggling now?
◆ Wrong key word	Zak has eight cakes. He gives three cakes to some friends. How many *more* cakes can he give to his friends?
◆ Two stage and superfluous information	Jon has twenty pairs of socks. Six pairs are blue. Four pairs are white. Two red pairs have holes in them. The other pairs are green. All his socks fit size 11 feet. If Jon gets three green pairs wet, how many pairs of green socks are dry?

Pupils can be guided towards increasing complexity and creativity, hopefully understanding how word problems are constructed.

In addition to coping with the flexibility of vocabulary for the four signs, +, −, ×, ÷, pupils will meet questions where the words are deliberately used to have an opposite meaning and again we are into semantics. They need a strategy that goes beyond just highlighting the key word and relating it to the usual operation.

For example, the pupils' task could be to write a word problem where a word such as 'more' is used first to infer addition and then second to infer subtraction. This is often a matter of just changing the order of the other words.

1   Jon has three toys. Sam has two more toys than Jon. How many toys does Sam have?

$$3 + 2 = 5$$

2   Sam has three toys. Sam has two more toys than Jon. How many toys does Jon have?

$$3 - 2 = 1$$

And using a different order for 'less':

3 Jon has three toys. Sam has two less toys that Jon. How many toys does Sam have?

$$3 - 2 = 1$$

4 Sam has three toys. Sam has two less toys than Jon. How many toys does Jon have?

$$3 + 2 = 5$$

Interpreting word problems

1 *Pictures* Because language is so variable and word problem writers are so creative (in a stilted sort of a way), one of the best strategies is to illustrate the problem with simple drawings.

Jon ✈✈✈	Sam ✈✈✈ + ✈✈
Jon . . . 3 toys	*Sam . . . Jon's toys (3) and 2 more makes 5*
Who has more toys?	*Sam*
Sam ✈✈✈	Jon ✈ (✈✈)
Sam . . . 3 toys	*Sam has two more toys than Jon, so Jon has 2 less*
Who has more toys?	*Sam*

The illustrations should be backed by the key question, 'Is the answer bigger or smaller?' now slightly rephrased as, 'Who has more toys (Jon or Sam)?'

2 *Reword the question* As in 'Who has more toys?'

3 *Selecting the operation(s)* As in 'Is this add, subtract, multiply or divide?'

4 *Throwing in a guesstimate and evaluating the outcome* Does it make sense?

Then there are the questions that not only require the student to decide on the operation, but also require them to apply commonsense. Many students do not relate maths questions to the same reality as a teacher, so in the example below, the question setter is anticipating $32 \div 5$ followed by rounding up 6.4 to 7. A 12 year old pupil wrote her answer as '32'. One could make an argument in support of that answer. So the commonsense that was required was as expected by the question setter, not the commonsense applied by the student.

◆ Sophisticated maths content   If cars take 5 people, how many cars would be needed to take a group of 32 friends to a concert?

Different shapes, different words: the vocabulary of shape and space

Some of the vocabulary around shape and space topics is quite exclusive, and hence perceived as alienating. For example, there are a number of words to describe different four sided shapes. Do these help pupils to understand what makes a shape different? For example, arrange these words in a logical sequence and then justify your decision.

QUADRILATERAL, SQUARE, TRAPEZIUM, RECTANGLE, PARALLELOGRAM, KITE, RHOMBUS

Now do the same for triangles.

ISOSCELES, EQUILATERAL, SCALENE, RIGHT ANGLED, ACUTE ANGLED, OBTUSE ANGLED

Links

Some words can be linked to meanings that are familiar, thus using the everyday/maths links as a help with the maths meaning. I have left space for your own and your pupils' link words and phrases.

centi century centipede centurian

_____

Circumference fence circling a field (see also perimeter)

_____

Complementary (angles) complete the straight line

_____

Concave going in to a cave

_____

Cosine (also sine and tangent) There are some well known 'poems' built around these and opposite, adjacent and hypotenuse. It would seem that the more inclined to innuendo, and the less subtle the content, the better the memory!

_____

Decagon decimal decade decimate

_____

Equi equal

Mega megastar

milli millennium millimetre (small)

Mode model, modern

Octagon octopus

Percentage per = divide   cent = hundred

Perimeter fence (and the per does not mean divide)

Quadrilateral quad bike

Speed (and velocity) can be linked via the units miles per hour or kilometres per hour – per means divide, both units have a distance unit divided by a time unit, so speed is distance ÷ time.

The instruction words

These need to be taught, demonstrated and explained. Pupils need to understand what they imply mathematically. They include:

calculate
compare
convert
correct (as in 'to 2 decimal places' and not as 'absolutely correct')
estimate
evaluate
expand
explain
express

factorise
find
invert
investigate
prove
round
simplify
solve

Conclusion

Communication via language is not as simple as it might seem. For example, some words used in maths come with a previously learned alternative meaning. The inconsistencies of vocabulary can confuse mathematically. As with many of the aspects of maths, assumptions are dangerous. With verbal communications and instructions, the assumption that what you say is what the learner hears may only be true at the literal level rather than at the understanding level.

Chapter 7

Anxiety and attributions

In many senses this is a chapter that brings together all the other chapters. If everything else about the learning is considered, for example, acknowledging weak short term memory, providing appropriate worksheets, anxiety, attitude and attribution can still generate failure. Failure can be specific to a topic, a lesson or even part of a lesson, but unaddressed, unrecognised failure at any stage in maths has serious consequences for future learning.

Maths seems to be *the* subject for creating anxiety. Books have been written about maths anxiety. I have known adults who have been driven close to depression by an unavoidable maths task. Even the memories of maths lessons can generate anxiety. A Danish friend remembers her maths lessons in school . . .

I am sitting in my room looking at the open maths book, getting ready to do my homework. All I can see are the numbers on the paper, numbers that frighten me and make me sad.

I keep sharpening my pencils again and again, constantly writing and erasing my answers making the pages in my maths book almost unreadable. Most of the pages are full of my teacher's red and blue notes. Everything I have written has been wrong.

The teacher's comments are filling as much space as are my attempts to please him and live up to his far too high expectations. I know that tomorrow I will again have to face humiliation in the classroom.

He will look at our homework and ask me questions he knows I cannot answer. I will try to make myself invisible again, but he will find me, asking me another impossible question. Everyone will look at me and he will say loudly, 'Let's ask someone who will know the answer.'

It is not what he is saying that hurts me, but it is his harsh voice, his hostile body language and angry expressions, his cold staring eyes, his angry stamping on the floor, his way of saying my name, his tight angry lips, the hard finger poking my back while he yells out loud, blaming me for not being able to do mathematics.

It's a scenario one hopes would be rare today, but maths anxiety doesn't always need so much extra help (!) from a teacher, the subject itself is enough for many learners. Within this story there are several important clues as to the influence of maths anxiety. It illustrates an interesting concept from Seligman, an American psychologist, the concept of 'Attributional Style'.

Let's take a closer look at this scenario.

> All I can see are the numbers on the page, numbers that frighten me and make me sad.

The visual impact of a page of numbers can be almost terrifying for some learners. They know that numbers relate to failure and a lot of numbers relate to a lot of failure. (I feel much the same about many of the forms I have to fill in as a Headteacher. Many people feel that way about their tax return.) The numbers also make her sad and that is a deeper emotion, more permanent.

> I keep sharpening my pencils again and again.

Busy work that delays starting work on the maths. (I do the same with those endless forms, but with me it's making coffee after coffee).

> constantly writing and erasing my answers

The learner is not committing to a final answer. Sometimes they will not commit to any answer at all, that is they just will not write anything.

> making the pages in my maths book almost unreadable.

Another way of avoiding producing work that can be marked as wrong, but risking further critical comments from a teacher.

> Most of the pages are full of my teacher's red and blue notes.

The teacher is giving feedback that confirms the learner's sense of inadequacy. I helped organise a conference for teenage dyslexic learners once. One of their recommendations for teachers was that they marked neatly, discretely and with a dark pen (that is not red). This negative feedback does not encourage pupils to take the risks necessary to become learners.

> Everything I have written has been wrong.

The learner feels that the problem is pervasive. *Everything* I have written. . . . This leads to a sense of helplessness.

> The teacher's comments are filling as much space as are my attempts to please him and live up to his far too high expectations.

Once again the feedback is reinforcing the learner's sense of inadequacy. This comment also introduces 'expectations'. Setting expectations at just the right level, not too low, not too high, and constantly adjusting them is a very demanding skill. Learners are surrounded by expectations, from governments through to peers. (One of the current words of UK education is 'targets', which is a word that seems to have taken on a meaning not dissimilar to expectations. It's not the word that is at fault, it is the interpretation used and the oversimplification of its application to situations that are totally inappropriate. Then there is a tendency to underestimate the impact of a badly interpreted idea.)

I know that tomorrow I will again have to face humiliation in the classroom.

The learner has a sense of pessimism and permanence.

The remaining two paragraphs graphically describe a person who is being taught by a teacher who should not be teaching. Every interaction described reinforces, powerfully, the helplessness of the learner. There is nothing to lead her out of her attributional style. The maths is no longer the issue.

The learner will start to form beliefs which then construct an attributional style that impacts on all future attempts to learn. For example:

I'm no good at maths. I never will be.

I can't do fractions. I can't do any maths.

I hate fractions. I hate all maths.

I don't read well. I'm hopeless at word problems.

People who like maths are weird.

I don't like maths. I don't know anyone who likes maths.

Only really clever people are good at maths (therefore I am not clever).

Anxiety

Anxiety is not always a bad thing. It is said that facilitative anxiety motivates and alters behaviour positively whereas debilitative anxiety inhibits or alters behaviour negatively, depending on the degree of anxiety and the make-up of the individual. However it is usually debilitative anxiety that we meet in maths.

Factors contributing to maths anxiety

It has been suggested that several factors may contribute to anxiety in maths, for example:

◆ A poor understanding of maths.
◆ The abstract nature of maths.
◆ Inappropriate instruction (instruction that does not differentiate for the range of learners in a group).

◆ Badly designed work tasks, for example, content beyond the learner's capabilities or messy, overcrowded worksheets.
◆ A curriculum that does not take account of the range of learners at whom it is targeted.
◆ Constant under-achievement.
◆ Teachers' attitudes.
◆ Parental attitudes.
◆ The pressure of having to do maths quickly.
◆ The extreme judgemental nature of maths, that is, answers are almost always judged as 'right' or 'wrong'.

The 'no answer'

In the 1990s I did a study on the errors that dyslexic secondary school pupils made in maths. A good example was 12.3 + 5, where the most common error was to add the .3 and the 5 to give an answer of 12.8. The percentage rate of this error was almost identical for the dyslexic pupils and the non-dyslexic pupils. The same was true for all computational errors in this no time limit test. The error that just stood out as different was the error of the no attempt. The pupil simply does not attempt the question. The answer space is left blank. Dyslexic pupils exhibited this reaction far, far more than the non-dyslexic pupils.

The reason was explained to me by a dyslexic pupil with a degree in maths: 'If I know I am going to fail to answer the question correctly, I don't try. Then no one can say to me, "Never mind, you did your best." If I do my best I want to succeed, not fail.'

Look for the no answers, the blank spaces in work. They are almost as diagnostic as the written or verbalised errors. An optimistic interpretation may mean the learner is insecure in that topic and it may be that all that is needed is a little review or reassurance. Of course it could also mean that the learner has a total blank on that topic, but at least you are taking a more refined diagnostic approach.

Risk taking

Most learning involves risk. A baby taking its first steps is taking a risk. Some people are natural risk takers across all aspects of their lives. Others have areas where they are natural risk takers but other areas where they are cautious to the 'no-attempt' level. For example I will take the risk of lecturing to a large audience, but I am firmly in the no-attempt camp for any roller coaster that does 360° loops.

It will be the classroom ethos that encourages or discourages risk taking in maths. The teacher that dramatically gives a large red ink cross across an incorrect question is not encouraging future risk taking. He has just upped the risk stakes for the learner. The teacher who says 'Close, just not quite right ... but close ... if you do this ... change this ... check that fact ... just read this bit again and tell me what you think it means,' or similar phrases, is encouraging risk taking.

The pupil who just sits there and is supremely reluctant to start work may well be an ultimate, but hopefully not terminal, risk avoider.

Risk taking and thinking style

A classroom study I was involved in, working in three European countries with 11–13 year old pupils with specific learning difficulties and non-spld controls, looked at their thinking styles in maths. The relevant finding for this chapter is that the spld group made very much more use of the formulaic inchworm style than their non-spld peers. We hypothesised that the reasons for this were that their conception of the inchworm style was that, even though it often made demands they could not handle, such as sequential memory, it seemed safer. Supporting this is the fact that the holistic and flexible grasshopper methods just offered too much choice and thus unacceptable insecurity.

The National Numeracy Strategy is encouraging pupils to generate different methods. This seems to be an international trend in maths curricula. But, as ever, there are implications in how it is done. Most importantly is an acceptance (active, not passive) by teachers that this can happen and a classroom ethos that encourages flexibility without frightening those pupils for whom flexibility is never going to be an option. I do not know what percentage this may be, I guess around 5 per cent, but inclusion encourages us to consider all children, not just the 67 per cent that are in the middle band of the normal distribution.

Expectations

Pupils are surrounded by many different sources of expectations. Some of these expectations may be conflicting, for example those of a peer group versus those of a teacher. Many pupils are adept at constantly adjusting to these surrounding and conflicting expectations. However there will be times when certain expectations take on a dominant role. Examinations are a prime example (see Figure 7.1).

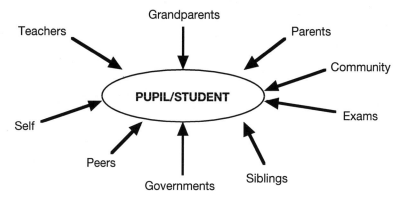

Figure 7.1 Expectations

Pupils are sometimes subject to expectations based on other family members. These may be verbalised by teachers. 'Your sister was just superb at maths,' or 'Your brother was useless at maths.' The pupil failing in maths may be all too aware of their successful (and even worse, younger) sibling.

There will be cultural expectations. A few years ago there was less expectation for females to do well in maths. A group of boys however may have a culture of not trying in maths. This may be partly to avoid failure whilst preserving an image, or it may be just rebellion or a result of the fact the group does not have an acceptable image of pupils who excel in maths.

In the current educational culture there is the fashion of setting targets, which are really just formally presented expectations. I have had concerns about this trend to set targets for individual pupils, mainly because this is such a very skilled task and subject to so many uncontrollable variables that (as a physicist) the accuracy of any target is dubious at best. Perhaps the Government's target should be that all children should be above average.

My starting analysis is that if the target is too easy, some learners will simply cruise, or worse, stop when they feel they have achieved the target. If the target is too high and unachievable then it demotivates. There are so many factors to consider and the learner does not provide a stable base. If he's tired, had a row with his girlfriend, his football team has lost or he's busy memorising the lyrics of a chart song, maths may not be the priority at that time. Wrapping up the whole process in mushy acronyms (for example, SMART) does not act as a substitute for appropriate training nor reduce the hazards associated with the process.

However, I do feel that expectations are the key to success. It's just that the bureaucrats have hijacked the idea. Expectations are linked, among other things, to attributional style. Teachers need positive, encouraging, nurturing attributions and they need to communicate them to their learners in a way that permeates all of their lessons. Expectations are fluid and adjustable. They often need on-going fine tuning if they are to be achieved and exceeded. So, when you write a target or an expectation, let the child and the circumstances dictate the outcome and then manage the consequences of that outcome.

So expectations or targets can be set at a whole school level, a year group level, a classroom level and an individual level. Statistically, each will be different in format and expected outcomes, but they should be complementary.

Beliefs and maths

There are many beliefs around maths. These tend to be rooted in early experiences, for example in early experiences of subtraction, children may be told 'You take the little number from the big number' which is a belief with a limited future. Some examples of beliefs are:

◆ Mathematics problems have only one answer (but the possibility of more than one answer creates a sense of uncertainty for some learners).
◆ In maths word problems, the relative size of numbers is more important than the relationships between the quantities they represent. (So, if the numbers are relatively close in value they are added or subtracted. If they are relatively far apart in value then they are multiplied or divided.)
◆ Mathematics is a collection of facts, rules, procedures and formulas (which is sometimes the way it is taught and sometimes the way it is perceived).
◆ You have to be really brainy to do maths (and thus 'not normal').
◆ Some learners see beliefs as inviolate, others see them as a challenge. As ever, the individual does not have to match the 'average'.

Anxiety, self confidence and attributional style: intervention and prevention

Addressing anxiety, self confidence and a negative attributional style is not likely to be a quick process. The chances are that the problem has built up over a long time and that it will only be reduced over a long time. There are some basic classroom strategies/philosophies for promoting pupils' self confidence in learning maths and thus guide their attributional style to be more optimistic and positive:

✔ Tell pupils that effort is important (learned-helpless pupils believe there is little relationship between effort and success) and then make sure that you reinforce this in comments, marking and any feedback to the pupil.

✔ Tell pupils that their own improvement is more important than doing better than other pupils.

✔ Make sure pupils experience genuine success in maths and avoid patronising praise.

✔ Give challenging tasks that show that being wrong is a part of the learning process, but control the impact of the mistakes by direct and personal encouragement. Trial and adjust questions are a relatively secure way of doing this. Some coursework can teach this lesson. Again some security and intervention may be needed.

✔ Promote pupil's self confidence in learning maths by giving positive and constructive feedback.

✔ Create a classroom ethos which encourages involvement, by:

   ✔ creating an ethos of meaningful praise (I prefer lots of 'little praises' to fewer 'big praises'; and
   ✔ creating an ethos that encourages learners to take a risk.

✔ Remind pupils that learning involves risk and make sure that the consequences of taking a risk are not negative.

An interesting thought: Do we teach algebra so that each new generation can share a common experience in maths, that is 'I can't do algebra!' (though I guess the same could be said of fractions).

Attributional style

Building a positive attributional style appeals to me as a more robust target than just building self esteem or self confidence. It seems to set firmer foundations and have a more lasting influence.

A poor attributional style is the result of constant negative feedback, perhaps internal as well as external, something that is more than likely for a weak maths student. The negative feedback comes from many sources: the teacher, in what he says and how he says it, in what he doesn't say, how he marks and appraises work; peers and the learner's status within the peer group; parents reactions to reports; and the learner's own frustrations and failures, real or imagined.

Seligman's interpretation of how people attribute their successes and failures is so apposite for maths learning. The three aspects of attribution are:

Pervasive   'I can't do this sum, I can't do any maths.'
Permanent 'I couldn't learn the times table facts last night. I'll never be able to learn them.'
Personal   'It's all my fault, I'm just thick.'

It takes time and that constant drip, drip of negative feedback to make attributions become negative, so it should be no surprise that it takes time and a lot of positive drips to turn those attributions around.

To sum up

This could be the most important topic in this book. Maybe more so with maths than with other subjects, the learner has to believe that he can do it or at the least make an attempt that will be genuinely valued. Self concept, self esteem, optimism and pessimism are concepts which we often discuss, but do we, as teachers keep them uppermost in our minds at all times. Sports managers pay big money to get their teams motivated and believing that they will win because they know how important those beliefs are to success, however skilled the team.

Chapter 8

The inconsistencies of maths

Another general factor to consider for uncertain learners is inconsistency. This may be a change of teacher, a new topic, a different room or inconsistencies in the subject. This short chapter tries to help teachers and support assistants gain an extra understanding of this facet of maths and how it may confuse insecure pupils. We try to encourage pupils to look for patterns and this is generally sound practice, but then we must be aware of the exceptions and the confusions that may arise as a consequence.

When I first started teaching mathematics I would say to my students, 'Maths is much better than spelling because in maths a rule is a rule, no exceptions!' But if you teach pupils who have problems in learning maths you learn to make no assumptions and to question everything you might have taken for granted even, for example, the 'simple' process of counting to twenty.

I began to recognise two important elements in teaching maths to my pupils. One was that maths has far more inconsistencies than I realised[1] and the other was that students who find learning maths difficult need and rely on consistency. If there are inconsistencies then we as teachers have to be aware of them and help our students to manage them.

Then I thought about the interaction of pupils' confusions arising from these inconsistencies and some research from eighty years ago.

Back in the 1920s two Americans, Buswell and Judd[2] wrote a monograph about teaching arithmetic. I have always felt that one of their observations is vitally important for learners (and teachers). Basically Buswell and Judd said that when you learn a new topic in arithmetic, if your first experience in practising and applying this new topic is incorrect, that inaccuracy becomes a dominant memory. So, for example, if despite careful teaching, the pupil adds $\frac{1}{20} + \frac{1}{20}$ as $\frac{2}{40}$, that procedural inaccuracy becomes what he remembers when faced with similar questions in future.

So the inconsistencies of maths may lead to inaccurate first experiences and we as teachers have to be aware of this and try to pre-empt the confusion or at least check pupils' initial practises quickly before any misunderstanding becomes embedded in our learners' minds.

We need to monitor and utilise the power of the first learning experience.

Some of the inconsistencies which can create confusion for learners are listed below. Being aware of these may also aid diagnosis (Chapter 9). Confusion over inconsistencies may be the root of other problems.

The inconsistencies which may lead to future confusions in maths start in very early numeracy, for example and, as already mentioned, in counting to twenty.

◆ We write numbers as 1, 2, 3, 4, 5, 6, 7, 8, 9 which are getting bigger as we write from left to right, then we write 11, 12, 13, 14, 15, 16, 17, 18, 19 where the bigger (value) digit is now on the left, even though it has been smaller in the earlier learning experience.

◆ The words for the teen numbers defy the convention used for other two digit numbers by referring to the unit digit first, thus thirteen compares badly with twenty three, thirty three and so on.

◆ Whilst we become regular in language structure for numbers in the hundreds and above using, for example, five hundred, five thousand and five million, we use fifty, which is not only not fivety, but is not five ten. (Maybe this has something to do with the history of the language of maths and the lower frequency of use of the higher numbers giving less chance for them to become colloquial.)

◆ Children are likely to meet 'third' and 'fourth' first (!) when used to denote order. Later the same words refer to fractions.

◆ We have a whole range of words to infer addition, subtraction, multiplication and division. For example 'more, plus, and, add' infer addition. So we can teach this flexibility in language and create classic maths word problems such as:

> Mark has eight pens. James has two more pens than Mark. How many pens does James have?

Then we use 'more' to mean 'subtract' as in:

> Mark has eight pens. Mark has two more pens than James. How many pens does James have?

◆ We 'carry' in addition sums and 'decompose' in subtraction sums, yet both are trading actions, trading ten ones for one ten and trading one ten for ten ones. (And decomposition is one of those words that has a meaning outside mathematics.)

◆ In early experiences of subtraction, the small is subtracted from the big. This does not remain a reliable concept.

◆ Multiplying may be taught as a process that makes things bigger, yet multiplying by $\frac{1}{2}$, $\frac{2}{3}$, 0.6 and so forth makes things smaller. (Similar confusing things happen with division.)

♦ We (normally) add, subtract and multiply in writing from units, through tens to hundreds and on, that is from right to left, but we divide from left to right and thus from thousands, to hundreds, tens and units. We may also add and subtract mentally starting from highest place value.

♦ For numbers and algebra,

> *a times b* equals *b times a* ($ab = ba$) for example $3 \times 4 = 4 \times 3$

> *a plus b* equals *b plus a* ($a + b = b + a$) for example $3 + 4 = 4 + 3$

but

> *a divided by b* does not equal *b divided by a* ($a/b \neq b/a$)
> for example $\frac{2}{3} \neq \frac{3}{2}$

> *a minus b* does not equal *b minus a* ($a - b \neq b - a$)
> for example $2 - 3 \neq 3 - 2$

♦ We expect absolute accuracy in numerical computations and then expect students to abandon this strict regime when learning to estimate.

♦ We teach place value and say 3456 as 'three thousand, four hundred and fifty six' but pupils' first experience of a four digit number is likely to be a year, for example, 1980, which we say as 'nineteen eighty' or 1066 which we say as 'ten sixty six'.

♦ ·In fractions the most familiar (and therefore the most useful, potentially, for teaching) are the two inconsistently named fractions, half and quarter. A third is OK as is a fifth, sixth and so on.

♦ In fractions big becomes small. For example $\frac{1}{9}$ is smaller than $\frac{1}{2}$.

♦ Again, in fractions we modify the use of the addition sign so, for example in

$$\frac{1}{5} + \frac{3}{5} = \frac{4}{5}$$

only the 'top' numbers are added.

Then we change again so that in multiplications such as

$$\frac{2}{5} \times \frac{3}{5} = \frac{6}{25}$$

both 'top' and 'bottom' numbers are multiplied.

♦ In whole numbers the sequence of words for the place values going from left to right of the decimal point is units, tens, hundreds, thousands. For decimals, the sequence from right to left of the decimal point is is tenths, hundredths, thousandths, which is a very subtle difference in sounds, but a big difference in concept.

- With angles we tend to measure anti-clockwise, but with time we work clockwise.

- There are 90° in a right angle (would 100° cause fewer problems?), and what about a campaign to change the 12 hours for a half day to 10 (just joking, don't tell the EC).

- Time works with 12 and 60 instead of 10 and 100 and is cyclical, that is we count up to 12 (sometimes 24 to add more confusion) and 60 and then start at 1 again. We do this with days (in 7s) and months (in 12s) too and weeks are in 52s.

- With time we count on from the hour until half past, then we count down to the next hour. So 4:30 is 'four thirty', but 4:50 is 'ten to five' (4:50 having neither a five nor a ten).

- Even 7:10 can be verbalised as 'seven ten' which has the words in the same order as the numbers or as 'ten past seven' which has the words in reverse order.

- The basic unit of length is the metre, m. The basic unit of volume is the litre, l. The basic unit of mass is the kilogram, kg, not the gram, g.

- In measurement 'm' means metre, mile and milli (but not mega and micro).

- Children are often told that multiplying a number by 1 does not change the number, yet in fractions, for example

$$\frac{2}{3} \times \frac{5}{5} = \frac{10}{15}$$

$\frac{10}{15}$ is the same *value* as $\frac{2}{3}$ but certainly does not look the same.

- In algebra we use x to mean 'any number'. Then we give pupils $2x + 8 = 20$, and ask them to find a particular number value for x.

- And in arithmetic $\times$ has always meant multiply, now in algebra it doesn't and further than this in algebra we omit any symbol for multiply.

- 'Remove the brackets' as in $(y + 3)(y - 5)$ is not meant literally.

- In calculus the dy (and dx) in dy/dx does not mean d times y and d times x.

- In trigonometry $\sin^{-1}$ does not mean $\frac{1}{\sin}$.

- In algebra we keep the symbols $+$ and $-$ but lose $\times$ and $\div$.

This list is just a few examples. As time goes by and I teach each new class, I learn new things and I continue to add to my list of inconsistencies. My students continue to teach me about understanding maths. Teaching is always about learning.

When he was a young man the Nobel Prize winning scientist Richard Feynman invented his own symbols for trigonometry, calculus and other areas of maths, which were to him far more consistent than the traditional symbols (for example in d*x*/d*y* he was tempted to cancel the d's). Unfortunately reality intervened and he realised that to communicate with other mathematicians he had to use the same symbols as them. So I guess reality will have to rule here, too and we will have to accept and work with the inconsistencies.

Just to complete the chapter I have reproduced an article, obviously written very tongue in cheek, that was published originally in *Mathematics Teaching*, a journal of the Association of Teachers of Mathematics (ATM), number 175, June 2001, pp. 12–13. It is reprinted with ATM permission.

It was just a matter of time

Old Dr Algy B'rah faced the Lower Third maths class for lesson 10 on Friday afternoon.

'Now, today, or perhaps it was yesterday, when I said it would be tomorrow. In fact sometime recently I said that it was about time I spent some time teaching you time.

Time is easy to understand and to help I've brought in a real clock. This is the clock face. You'll see that it doesn't have eyes or a nose but it does have hands. Unlike you there are three hands to one face. The first hand is the hour hand, the second hand is the minute hand and the third hand is the second hand. Is that clear?

The little hand is the hour hand and the big hand is the minute hand. That's minute not minute, otherwise it wouldn't be big would it?

There are numbers round the clock face. They start with 1, which is not the number at the top and go round to 12 which is at the top. This is because there are 24 hours in a day. So there are 24 hours in a day and we put 12 of them on a clock and use them twice.

See all these little marks. They are the marks for minutes which can also be used for seconds and there are 60 of those, so 1 means 1 if it's hours and 5 if it's minutes and 5 if it's seconds and 2 means 10 minutes when it's not hours and 10 seconds when it's not minutes. So there are 60 minutes in an hour and 60 seconds in a minute and we only use them once, not twice like hours.

When the big hand is pointing at 12 and the little hand is pointing at 4 it is four o'clock. No it isn't really 4 o'clock now, sit down, and no, Seamus, o'clock is not an Irish name.

The hands go round and round and round. It is all very logical. It takes the hour hand half a day to go round. It takes the minute hand an hour to go round and it takes the second hand a minute to go round. And when the hour hand has been round twice it's tomorrow and today becomes yesterday.

Now, when we start to go past o'clock, we get to times like 5 past 1, which we write as 1.05. This means the little hand starts to move away from the 1 and the minute hand moves away from the 12. The little hand heads for 2 and the big, minute hand moves away from the 12, which also means zero, but it doesn't say it, and heads for the 1 which also means 5. This goes until

30 past 1, which is also half past 1, which is also 1.30, but the . is not a decimal and 30 is not the decimal .30 which is $\frac{3}{10}$ but now it's $\frac{1}{2}$, not .50 so we have to remember that $\frac{1}{2}$ can be written as .30, but if you do that with decimal numbers I will mark it wrong. Then we say 25 to 2, which is not tutu or to to or two two and 20 to 2 and quarter to 2 and 10 to 2. Of course 20 to 2 could be one third to 2, but that would be difficult so we don't say that, because we want time to be easy. And of course 20 to 2 could be one forty, which is not the same as forty one backwards, because we always say the hour first except when we say it second after the minutes. And the to is not two or 10 to 2 would be 1022 which is forty four years before the Battle of Hastings.

So we count in minutes after the hour, but only until 30 minutes after the hour, then we count down to the next hour, even though the minute hand is now moving up, except when we use times like 1.35. This means we change the hour we are talking about at half past the first hour and use the next hour half an hour before we reach the next hour. Once you think about that it all becomes clear, doesn't it?

Now you have all that clear we can move on to the 24 hour clock which is used for trains, buses and aeroplanes, all examples where you really need to know time to be on time. We still use the 12 hour clock face I've shown you but when we go round the second time with the hour hand we now have to remember that for the 24 hour clock 1 means 13, 2 is 14, 3 is 15 and so on. So the 1 on the clock face can mean 1 for hours, 13 for hours, 5 for minutes and 5 for seconds. When we get past 6 numbers like 9 can mean 9, 21, 45 or $\frac{1}{4}$ and 7 can mean 7, 19, 35 or 25. And don't forget that $10 + 5 = 3$ with the 12 hour clock and $10 + 5 = 15$ with the 24 hour clock and $23 + 8 = 07$ with the 24 hour clock and I know we haven't written 0 in front of a whole number before.

On the 24 hour clock after times like fifteen fifty nine we go to sixteen hundred, which is really fifteen sixty, but after 59 we go back to zero again and call it hundred. This means we have to remember that 20.40 is not the same as 20.40 in decimals but is the same as 8.40 and 20 to 9. That's clear to me, so it should be clear to you.

I just can't understand why you can't do time. No I don't mean "do time" as in "doing time" Bodger.'

And we expect young children to understand time!

Learners who are insecure or uncertain do not handle inconsistencies well. Time is full of inconsistencies, in the vocabulary used and in the way numbers are used.

Chapter 9

Assessment and diagnosis

Assessment and diagnosis

There are some good arguments for making this the first chapter. Obviously one could ask 'How can you remediate before you diagnose?' Well. I've put this chapter almost at the end of the book on the basis that it is not possible to diagnose until you understand the problems.

Let me define how I see assessment and diagnosis.

Assessment is about measuring the student's achievements, skills and deficits.

Diagnosis is about understanding why a student is not learning or why he is underachieving and should also lead to advice on how to teach him.

Assessment and diagnosis should always be interlinked and both should be ongoing. Both can be used to identify problems and possibly lead to ideas for addressing the problems, but, more importantly in my opinion, both can be used to pre-empt many problems. As far as is possible we need to get teaching right first time to capture the powerful influence of the first learning experience.

Assessment

Assessment may be via a standardised test or a national test (for example GCSE) or a school-based test. That is to say, an assessment is often one outcome from specifically chosen maths tasks, usually in the form of a test or examination which are specifically designed to measure the current achievement levels of the student. This is often measured in comparison with other pupils.

A standardised test is a test which has been trialled on a suitably large sample of typical subjects and then the scores are examined, items are modified or exchanged, until the test results are statistically satisfactory. Usually this means they fit a normal (bell shaped) distribution. A teacher using the test can then compare his pupils' results with the standardised results. This should give a measure as to how far ahead or behind a pupil's performance is compared to his peers. Standardised tests are usually used to measure progress (but see later) or the current state of pupils' learning and achievement.

In summary, then, what standardised testing does is to give a 'maths age' either as a one-off or for monitoring progress. Some standardised tests also encourage diagnostic interpretation, though this will inevitably be much less than would be obtained from an individual assessment.

I feel that it should be obligatory that testing should have an outcome that is beneficial to the learner, whether it is in identifying blocks to learning, directing additional intervention to the learner or directing extra resources to the learner. Then just how the information/results of the test are given (or not) to the learner may take him forward or set him back.

The following Checklist may help you select a standardised test.

Checklist for standardised tests

◆ Is it a test which is restricted in use to psychologists? (For example the WOND, the Weschler Objectives Numerical Dimensions may only be used by psychologists.)

◆ How much does it cost (a) initially and (b) for extra test sheets and score sheets?

◆ What does it look like? (For example, are the items too close together? Is the type clear?)

◆ How long does it take? (There will be a compromise between a test being thorough enough to give a valid measurement and being too daunting usually by demanding too long a concentration time from the subject and often consuming too much teaching time.)

◆ What is the target age range? (A small age range may make comparisons more accurate, but may handicap long term monitoring.)

◆ Can it be read to pupils? (You're testing maths not reading. However, reading the test to the student may invalidate the use of the standardised results.)

◆ How many items for a one year gain of maths age? (One year's progress could be just two items, but usually is about five.)

◆ How often do you wish to assess progress? Does the test have a parallel form? (These questions follow on from the previous question.)

◆ Does it match your maths curriculum? (Are you testing what your students have been taught?)

◆ Do the individual items test what they are intended to test? (For example 33×251 may test long multiplication, whereas 79×683 may only expose inadequate recall of times tables facts.)

◆ Can you extract any diagnostic information? (The answer to this question is usually 'Yes', even if the information only starts your diagnosis.)

◆ What are the details of the standardising sample? (How large? What is the make-up? Any special needs? etc.)

◆ Is there a balanced mix of thinking/cognitive styles of the questions?

Remember that testing is not an exact science, particularly when interpreting the test results from one individual. Pupil's attitudes and performances may be labile. You could have set the test on a bad day for a pupil. Also an average score for a group may mask many individual variations. (Averages do worry me!)

Having chosen your test, using it will confirm, or disprove your choice. Sometimes use with pupils will be the only way to make the final decision. Of course, syllabus changes may make your choice redundant, but this may not be so, for example, despite the radical approach of the National Numeracy Strategy the actual maths content is much as it ever was. This is usually the situation (with the possible exception of the somewhat bizarre foray into 'new' maths some years ago which destroyed what remained of parental confidence in trying to help children with maths).

I was privileged to hear Alan Kaufman a world expert on testing, speak at a conference in Sweden in 2002. I asked if I could use the following quote from his talk, which I think summarises what a tester should always have in mind,

'Be better than the test you use.'

How often should standardised tests be used?

There are tests which are designed to be pre- and post- (intervention or teaching programme) tests. The time span is then defined. The frequency with which other tests are used should depend partly on the number of items that create a twelve month gain. Some tests are time consuming and this may affect frequency of use.[1] Basically using standardised testing once a year is sensible, but there is a but.

When to use a standardised test

But in order to compare gains made over twelve months, you may have to test twice a year. The summer break is a great opportunity for maths skills and knowledge to slip back and thus for test scores to decay. Maths is a set of skills and, like any skill, performance will deteriorate in the absence of practise. Therefore, any testing done at the start of the academic year is likely to show lower performance scores from tests done at the end of the academic year.

Testing at the end of the academic year should show the maximum score for any individual, but it will be too late to be of diagnostic value in terms of guiding intervention.

A good compromise may be to test at the start of the academic year, when the test should provide good diagnostic information, both for individuals and for the class group, by highlighting weaker areas which can then be addressed before new work is introduced. The areas which have declined over the summer break may well be areas where learning is fragile and thus in need of top-up revision. By analysing as a group and as individuals, intervention can be delivered more effectively and efficiently. For example, if, say 60 per cent of the group show a weakness in a particular topic then a group intervention is efficient. If only 5 per cent of the group show a problem in a particular task, then more individualised intervention is appropriate.

And then test half way through the year which will show mid-year progress (though remember just how discriminating your test really is) and show if the deficits have been rectified. Test scores over equivalent twelve month periods may then be compared as measures of progress.

Summary

✔ Test at the start of the academic year.

- Analyse the results to show areas of weakness in the class group and in individuals. Plan interventions.

✔ Test mid-year to indicate the progress of individuals and the group.

- Analyse the results for the group and for individuals to show patterns of strength and weakness.

✔ Compare results for twelve month intervals to show progress from mid-year to mid-year and start of year to start of year.

Remember that testing is not an exact science, particularly when interpreting the test results from one individual. Pupil's attitudes and performances may be labile. You could have set the test on a bad day for a pupil. Also an average score for a group may mask many individual variations. Remember that a class does not have enough pupils to allow for statistical significance, for example, to be a normal distribution.

Remember, beware the average.

Diagnosis

Diagnosis is usually the outcome from examining the work and/or working with an individual. It relies on empathetic observation skills, a good understanding of maths and an even better understanding of the learner.

It is possible to extract diagnostic information from almost any maths work, but the amount and accuracy of your diagnosis will increase dramatically if you are able to see the learner working and can ask questions as he works. Sometimes errors are obvious (for example $32.6 - 4 = 32.2$). Sometimes they are impossible to identify unless you can ask the key diagnostic question, 'Tell me how you did that,' or encourage the student, 'Can you talk me through your method?'

I am a great believer in *informal diagnosis*. Informal diagnosis does not necessarily mean sitting down with the learner for an hour or more going through a lot of worksheets and tests on maths. It could be an ongoing process with information coming from occasional questions, possibly prompted by marked work, slowly building the picture, but also influencing and changing that picture with interventions following on from the diagnosis. As a (lapsed) chemist I recall my understanding of the Heisenberg principle which stated that whatever you measure, in doing the measurement you change what you measure (and sometimes in this particular setting change can be a good thing).

So you can extract diagnostic information from pre-set tests such as the Key Stage tests or a standardised test, but this will obviously be restricted to information around the content of the test. You may wish to have information that is not covered by the test and that will be addressed a little later in this chapter.

Why do you test? Some reasons for testing

When teachers ask me 'What test do you recommend?' I ask 'What do you want to find?' and maybe 'Why are you testing?' (I realise the answer to the second question may well be 'Because X told me to.')

There are a number of reasons why we test.

- A teacher may wish to monitor the progress of his or her group and/or identify those who need extra help and/or collect data with which to stream groups.
- Parents may wish to know how their child's achievements compare with those of his peers.
- There may be a need to measure rates of progress.
- To evaluate the maths programme.
- There may be some mandatory requirement to test.
- The test may be used to assess the ability of the pupil to progress to higher levels of study or to a new school.
- To provide information for an educational statement of special needs (which may be the same as the previous item).
- The test may be used to award a certificate recording a level of achievement (for example, GCSE or National Curriculum Key Stage 4).
- It may be used for diagnostic reasons (for example, to find the student's strengths, weaknesses, knowledge base and learning style).
- To provide information which will guide the teaching of the student.

Some basic questions: the overview

What do you want to know? Why do you want to know it?

How big is the problem?	A mathematics age.
What can't he do?	For example, procedures, language, recall, speed.
What can he do?	Recall facts, compensatory strategies, concepts.
What doesn't he know?	Basic facts, procedures, concepts.
What does he know?	Basic facts, procedures, concepts.
How does he learn?	Cognitive style, learning style, use of materials.
How can I teach him?	Cognitive style, learning style, use of materials.
What does he bring?	Attitude, anxiety, beliefs, history.
Where do I start the intervention?	The key question, but usually further back than you think.

Basic information and informal testing

What are the fundamental skills and knowledge learners need to start arithmetic and thus move on to numeracy and mathematics? I would be a brave man if I tried to provide the definitive answer to that question, but there are some basic topics that must be keys to progress. These include awareness of number values, a knowledge of basic facts and the four operations and an ability to take number manipulations beyond counting. Obviously the age of the person will have some influence on what is asked and how it is asked. The questions might cover:

◆ recognition of groups of dots, regularly and randomly arranged;
◆ counting/adding tasks and number bonds (particularly for 10);
◆ a short term memory test, for example digit span;
◆ multiplication facts;
◆ place value;
◆ mathematical vocabulary;
◆ the four operations (+, −, ×, ÷) and error patterns;
◆ money (possibly plus decimals and fractions – but be aware of anxiety);
◆ word problems;
◆ thinking style;
◆ attitude and anxiety.

Informal diagnostic testing should:

◆ follow clues from the standardised testing;
◆ focus in on specific problems, e.g. recall of facts or reading problems;
◆ relate to the subject's needs in maths;
◆ 'follow' the pupil/subject (so maybe not all factors have to be investigated);
◆ look for and identify error patterns;
◆ lead to suggestions for remediation specific to the person;
◆ be low stress;
◆ involve a mix of direct questions ('How are you getting on with learning the times tables?', 'Would you explain your work for that problem, please?') and 'doing' maths (use mini-worksheets or flash cards);
◆ be aware of the non-verbal factors.

Seating for testing

You need to sit where you can see the subject and you need to be familiar with the tests you use so that you can observe the subject as he works in order to pick up all the non-verbal clues such as finger counting, sub-vocalising and anxiety. (See Figure 9.1.)

Some informal tests using simple materials

These make good warm up questions for an individual diagnosis as they are relatively low stress.

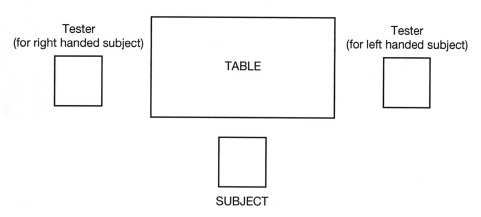

Figure 9.1 Seating for the assessment

◆ Throw about thirty or forty penny coins (or matches) on a table and ask the subject to estimate the number. Then ask him to count the coins.

> The estimation exercise gives you some idea about the subject's sense of number.

> The counting checks one-to-one correspondence. Also it is of interest to see how the subject counts. Does he simply count or does he arrange or pile the coins in fives or tens or use some grouping of numbers?

◆ Give the subject about twenty-three penny coins and three or four 10p coins. Ask him to give you 9p. If he gives you nine 1p coins ask for another 9p and then again. He does not have enough penny coins for the third 9p so does he offer a 10p and ask for change? Does he ask you to change a 10p coin for ten one pence coins? Does he say he can't because he doesn't have nine one pence coins. You are exploring his sense of units and tens in terms of a familiar material, money and thus the foundation of place value.

◆ Give the subject ten 1p coins. Split them as 5 and 5 (in a line). Write 5 + 5 = 10 on paper. Ask the pupil to write other pairs of numbers which add to 10. Tell him he may use the coins to help if he wishes.

> You are observing if he does need the coins or whether he can just work with the written digits. (And you can question him to make sure he is not just using the coins to humour you.) You are also observing how he organises this 'number bonds for 10' task. Is he random? Does he just do half (that is 6 + 4 and not 4 + 6)? The exercise extracts information about these key facts in a somewhat less stressful manner and in a way that gives some hint as to underlying understanding of the pattern involved.

◆ Give the subject twenty-four 1p coins. Ask him to share them equally between two people, then four people.

> How is the sharing done? One by one? Does he count the total, divide by two mentally and then count out twelve? Does he group the coins in fives

or tens? When you ask him to share between four people, does he start again with the twenty-four or does he half the groups of twelve?

◆ Ask the subject, 'What is a half of fifty?' Sometime later show him a card on which is written $\frac{1}{2} \times 50 = \square$ and, without reading out the card ask him 'What is the answer?' It's a crude test of the difference in understanding spoken maths and written, symbolic maths. You can adjust the question for younger children.

Recognising groups of dots

This is to check if the subject has any sense of the size, names and the values of numbers. Most adults can recognise (without counting) five, six or seven randomly arranged objects. Younger children less. A series of cards on which dots are printed should be available for use, for example the eight cards in Figure 9.2. Cards A to E could be used for checking recognition or counting. E and F could be used to ask if the subject can tell which card has more dots. Cards E and G could be used to check if counting skills are affected by random arrangements of dots. Card H could be used to check if patterns are recognised (2 × 4).

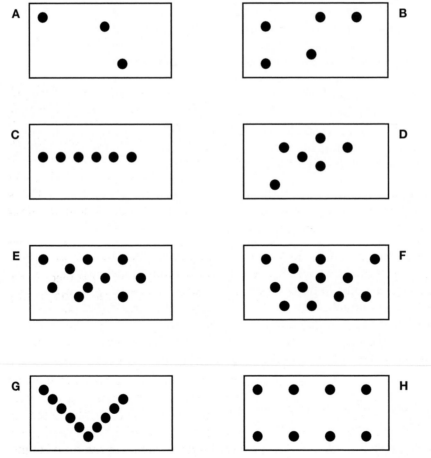

Figure 9.2 Dot recognition and counting

Counting and adding tasks

Ask the subject to count out twenty-two coins. Check for one-to-one correspondence and grouping (as a means of checking).

Show the subject cards with simple addition sums:

4 + 3 = ?   to check for accuracy and method. Does he start to count at 4 instead of 5? Does he 'just know', does he relate this to 3 + 3 or 4 + 4?

3 + 8 = ?   to check if he adds 8 onto 3 or 3 onto 8, that is does he overview before counting and appraise the task?

5 + 5 = 10   and ask if he can write some other pairs (two) of numbers that add up to ten. Check for any systematic approach and whether he appreciates the link between 3 + 7 and 7 + 3. If the subject is hesitant with the written task, give him ten coins to help work out the answers. This will tell you if the subject knows these essential facts and how he accesses them.

5 + 6 = ?   to see if he inter-relates the ten bonds to other facts. You could also try 7 + 8 = ?

4 + □ = 11   to check if the subject knows how to approach number bonds when written in a different format. Does he relate 4 + 7 to 4 + 6 = 10?

It is possible to check recall of addition and subtraction facts informally by simply asking the answers to a few random questions. It is worth asking how they knew the answer (recall or strategy). It will be interesting to compare recall of addition facts with recall of subtraction facts (which may indicate the level of confidence with which these facts are known). Watch for subtle counting techniques such as counting objects in the room (eye movements give this away) or almost imperceptible movements of fingers resting on their leg. Less subtle are the pupils who tap their nose or chin as they count, which truly is an early stage of approaching and using number.

An alternative or supplementary approach is to ask some specific facts under instant recall conditions and then later with 12 second intervals to find an answer in order to see if the facts just cannot be accessed at all or if the subject has a process that takes him to an answer. These processes often indicate good facility with numbers, though this is less likely if the strategy is finger counting.

Short term memory

There are standardised tests for short term memory, but you just need to have an idea of how many items the subject can handle rather than comparing him with his peers. So ask him to repeat the digits that you say, and then say, at one second intervals, two digits (for example 7 4), three digits, four digits, five digits, six digits (for example 3 8 7 1 3 5). If he fails at any point give another set of digits, if he fails again abandon the test.

It may be worth doing an extension by saying digits and asking the subject to repeat them in reverse order, for example, you say 5 1 8 and he says 8 1 5. This gives you an indication of how many items of data the subject can deal with at one time. So, if he is limited to three, then numbers in the thousands may be too much for his memory to deal with. As an example of this, a colleague was working with a 14 year old student, asking him to extend the sequence *abcdeabcdeabc* ... His analysis was, '*abc, dea, bcd, eab* ... I can't see any pattern.' It was a five unit task for a student with a three unit memory.

Testing recall of multiplication facts

For the multiplication facts, I like to ask 'Which of the times tables do you think you know well?' Then ask a couple of random facts to check if the answer is obtained by recall or by using a linking strategy (for example counting on fingers in twos to achieve the answer to 7×2 or in 5s to answer 7×5). If recall is not good, for example if the subject cannot recall 3×8 or 6×6, try offering $2 \times 8 = 16$ or $5 \times 6 = 30$ as starting points to explore his use of links.

As with addition and subtraction facts, an alternative approach is to ask some specific facts under instant recall conditions and then later with 12 seconds to find an answer in order to see if the facts just cannot be accessed at all or if the subject has a process that takes him to an answer. These processes often indicate good facility with numbers.

Place value

Use a series of place value cards (see Figure 9.3) to ask what specific digits represent, 'What is the value of this number in this place?' Try asking what happens to a place value when the number is multiplied or divided by 10, 100 or 1000 to check deeper understanding.

Mathematical vocabulary

(See pp. 95–7.) What you ask will be very much dependent on the age and current achievement level of the subject and, also, of course on his reading level. This will demand a good degree of empathy if the subject is not to be embarrassed.

At a basic level you can ask what word could be used for each sign: +, −, ×, ÷, =, and then what other words he knows for each sign, to investigate how much flexibility he has in basic maths vocabulary. Then, showing a word, you should ask for the reverse translation as in 'Which maths symbol does this word normally mean?' You could have a set of cards, each with a maths sign, so that he can point to the symbol.

In Chapter 6 there is a list of instruction words which you could use to investigate the learner's understanding of key vocabulary.

The four operations: +, −, × and ÷

This could be a huge section, so you will need to target a level of question based on a simple screening test (such as Figure 9.4) or the results from the standardised

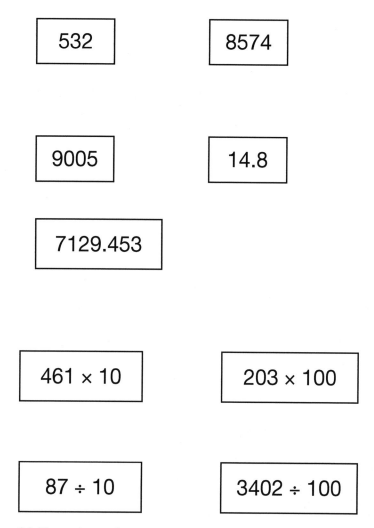

Figure 9.3 Place value cards

test used at the start of the diagnosis. Then it is a matter of setting up a set of criterion referenced tests such as in Appendix 5 to target the specific level of the subject and the demands of the maths he will be facing.

Look for errors and the questions which are not attempted. Make your own interpretations, but back them with, 'Tell me how you did this question.'

Errors

A quick and accurate performance with the four operations (+, −, ×, ÷) is an essential part of early mathematics and is one of the basic life skills. Children who are not able to perform accurately and swiftly on these questions are likely to be judged (not always correctly) as having poor potential in mathematics. Two of the factors affecting speed are quick access to basic facts and facility with the algorithms used to solve each question. Failure in either or both of these two areas will create slow and often inaccurate work. However, an ability to estimate and name ....   date ....

```
  16            308          12.3 + 5 =
 +27           +897
```

```
    19.09 + 10.91 =              63 + 2.1 =
```

```
   67          72          813          601
  −32         −48         −668         −346
```

```
    37.6 − 4 =              21.003 − 2.114 =
```

```
   6        60        33        44        202
  x5      x  5      x20      x21       x 25
```

```
  2)‾39          6040 ÷ 10 = 64          3)‾906
```

```
     5)‾668               15)‾345
```

Figure 9.4 Screening test for basic numeracy skills

evaluate answers may offer some compensation and give some support to confidence and accuracy.

Mathematics anxiety can be a contributing factor here, with children often tending not to try questions which they feel they are unable to complete successfully. The 'no answer' questions should also be part of the analysis.

The screening test (Figure 9.4) can be used as an initial test of speed of working, accuracy and errors. The test is used here to illustrate how diagnostic information can be extracted from almost any maths tests and how some common errors can be identified. The twenty-one questions in the screening test should be completed within 8 minutes for 11 to 13 year old pupils. Longer times should be considered to indicate a slow rate of work which is likely to handicap the subject, especially if a school pupil. Standardised tests, such as the WRAT (Wide Range Achievement Test) are also affected by speed and can be used to provide further information.

The test has not been statistically standardised to provide a mathematics 'age'. There are other tests in existence which do this such as the WISC, the Basic Number Screening Test, the Mathematics Competency Test (for test suppliers see Appendix 2). The tester should be looking for an overall impression of accuracy, errors and at the type of question which is answered incorrectly and not attempted as well as the questions which are answered accurately.

Surprisingly, one of the most telling reactions to a mathematics question is the 'no attempt'. A learner who deliberately does not try to solve a question is showing a lack of confidence, anxiety, a desire not to be wrong ('better not to try') and probably a real or self-perceived lack of skill. Examine the questions which are not attempted. There may be a pattern, for example, questions involving zeros or decimals. Again the pattern will be used when planning a remedial programme. A 'no answer' may well affect the time taken to finish attempting the test.

Consideration of the subject's error patterns is a most important part of the information gathered from a diagnosis. Error patterns often indicate the misunderstandings and incorrect procedures used by the subject. Intervention can then be accurately and appropriately targeted. Each item in the screening test has been considered separately, but inter-related errors and the overall pattern should also be considered. Some items have been included to interact and confirm patterns. For example, 12.3 + 5 and 37.6 − 4 test similar skills and concepts. Some items are part of a progression, especially in the multiplication section.

The Criterion referenced tests used in Appendix 5 can be used to provide further evidence of error patterns highlighted in the screening test (or any standardised test).

Although error patterns are discussed for each item, experience suggests that some subjects will make errors that have not been listed here. Sometimes an error will be inexplicable, even if you are in a position to ask the subject to explain. However, the most likely errors are listed. The error types are based on Engelhardt's classification:[2]

> Basic fact error
> Defective algorithm
> Grouping error
> Inappropriate inversion
> Incorrect operation
> Incomplete algorithm
> Zero error

Error analysis

Some errors may occur in every item and are not therefore listed each time in the following analysis. These errors are:

> basic fact errors
> wrong operation
> no attempt
> transposals

All errors are noteworthy, but special attention should also be given to the items which are not attempted. If possible, ask the subject why the item was not tried.

A possible error path is suggested for each wrong answer. There may be another explanation.

Addition items   1
$$\begin{array}{r} 16 \\ +27 \\ \hline 43 \end{array}$$

(This is a warm up item and is unlikely to generate an error. The basic errors described, however, could occur in any other item.)

44   Basic fact error, for example, computing $7 + 6$ as 14.
61   Transposal error, adding 7 and 6 as 13, but writing 1 in the units column and 'carrying' the 3 into the tens column.
313   Failure to 'carry' the 10 into the tens column.

2
$$\begin{array}{r} 302 \\ +897 \\ \hline 1199 \end{array}$$

1109   Zero error. Incorrect addition of $0 + 9 = 0$ in the tens column.

3    $12.3 + 5 = 17.3$

12.8   Decimal point error. The 5 unit is added to the 3 tenths.
62.3   Place value error. The 5 unit is added to the 1 from the tens place.
20   Concept error. The numbers are added as $12 + 3 + 5$. (This could also be a vision/reading problem.)

4    $19.09 + 10.91 = 30.00$

3000   The decimal point is omitted.

The item also generates zero errors and carrying errors. The item was included to test organisation of work, particularly the 'carrying' procedure.

5    $63 + 2.1 = 65.1$

This item is a variation on item (3), and errors made for the two items should be compared.

84   Decimal point error – 2.1 is added as 21.
8.4   Decimal point error – 63 is added as 6.3.
66   Concept error. The numbers are added as $63 + 2 + 1$.

Subtraction items   1
$$\begin{array}{r} 67 \\ -32 \\ \hline 35 \end{array}$$

Basic fact, and transposal errors.

It is also possible that, despite lining off the four sections of this test that the subject may perseverate and continue to add.

2   72
       −48
       ——
       24

     36   Inappropriate inversion. The 2 is subtracted from the 8.

3   813
     −668
     ——
     145

    255   Inappropriate inversion. The 3 is subtracted from the 8 and the 1 is subtracted from the 6.

    205   Zero error. The 1 is deleted for renaming into the units column, leaving a zero in the tens column. 0 − 6 is written as 0 (or possibly 6, giving 265).

4   601
    −346
    ——
    255

    305   Inappropriate inversion and zero error. The 1 is subtracted from the 6. Also a zero error. In the tens column 0 minus 4 is written as 0.

    365   Inappropriate inversion and zero error. The 1 is subtracted from the 6 and the 4 is subtracted from the 0, which has been interpreted as 10.

    265   Inappropriate inversion in the units column. Renaming in the tens column to give 10 − 4, leaving 5 − 3 = 2 in the hundreds column.

    345   Inappropriate inversions. The 1 is subtracted from the 6 and the 0 is subtracted from the 4.

5   37.6 − 4 = 33.6

    37.2   Decimal point error. The 4 units were subtracted from the 6 tenths.

    33.2   Decimal point error. The 4 was subtracted from the 6 tenths and the 7 units.

6   21.003 − 2.114 = 18.889

This item was included to test organisation of presentation and multiple use of the 'renaming/borrowing' procedure for subtraction. It can give rise to a wide range of errors, including zero errors. It is sufficiently complex to create organisation problems, with errors due to the subject simply losing their way in the middle of the problem.

19.111 Inappropriate inversion for the decimal numbers.

Multiplication items

1
$$\begin{array}{r} 6 \\ \times 5 \\ \hline 30 \end{array}$$

25 or 35   Basic fact error.

2
$$\begin{array}{r} 60 \\ \times\ 5 \\ \hline 300 \end{array}$$

305   Defective algorithm and zero error: $0 \times 5 = 5$ and $6 \times 5 = 30$.
30   Place value error
250   Basic fact error.

3
$$\begin{array}{r} 33 \\ \times 20 \\ \hline 660 \end{array}$$

600   Incomplete algorithm.
630   Defective algorithm and zero error. The subject writes down a 0, followed by $0 \times 3 = 3$ and $2 \times 3 = 6$
63   Defective algorithm: $0 \times 3 = 3$ and $2 \times 3 = 6$.
60   Incomplete algorithm and zero error.
66   Incomplete algorithm.

4
$$\begin{array}{r} 44 \\ \times 21 \\ \hline 924 \end{array}$$

As items become more complex, the range of possible errors increases enormously. The most frequent errors are listed.

84   Defective algorithm: $1 \times 4 = 4$ and $2 \times 4 = 8$.
8844   Grouping error: $1 \times 44 = 44$ and $2 \times 44 = 88$.
132   Defective algorithm: $1 \times 44 = 44$ which is added to 88 (from 2×44).

5
$$\begin{array}{r} 202 \\ \times\ 25 \\ \hline 5050 \end{array}$$

4010   Defective algorithm: $2 \times 5 = 10$ and $0 \times 2 = 0$ and $2 \times 2 = 4$.
410   Defective algorithm: $2 \times 5 = 10$ and $2 \times 2 = 4$.
100   Defective algorithm: $2 \times 25 = 50$ which is added to $2 \times 25 = 50$.
4050   Defective algorithm: $2 \times 25 = 50$ and $20 \times 2 = 40$.

Division
items

1   $2\overline{)39}$ = 19.5 or $19\frac{1}{2}$ or 19r1.

154r1   Defective algorithm: 30 ÷ 2 =15 and 9 ÷ 2 = 4r1.
18r1   Basic fact error.
14r1   Defective algorithm: 3 ÷ 2 = 1, the remaining 10 is not carried on to the 9 (making 19).

2   6040 ÷ 10 = 604

64   Obtained either by 60 ÷ 10 = 6 and 40 ÷ 10 = 4 or by missing out the 'middle' 0 when trying short division.

3   $3\overline{)906}$ = 302

32   Obtained by missing out the middle 0 when trying short division.

4   $5\overline{)668}$ = 133.6 or 133r3

111   Defective algorithm. No carried numbers used.

5   $15\overline{)345}$ = 23

20   Incomplete algorithm.

It is a relatively simple task to set your own error analysis tests, building up a resource of short and appropriate diagnostic tests for different stages of the curriculum.

Money

One of the behaviours teachers often notice is the way pupils can succeed when decimals have a £ sign in front of them. So, for example, if a pupil is faced with 14.4 + 5 he may well answer 14.9, but this is unlikely to be the answer when the question is £14.40 + £5.

Also money is truly life maths, so competence in this area is a very desirable outcome of education.

This section of the informal diagnosis could use coins and notes (real ones are best) as well as oral and written problems. A money sense of value could be checked by questions such as 'What is an approximate, easier value for £21.99?'

Word problems

There is an increasingly complex set of word problems in Chapter 6 which could act as a model for drawing up progressively more challenging word problems. You may only need to ask, 'Which operation would you use to solve this question?', but beware of the use of alternative methods and thus not the obvious operation, for example counting on instead of subtraction.

As with the vocabulary questions be empathetic enough to recognise reading problems and not embarrass the subject.

Thinking style

Not all pupils respond to the same methods of problem solving and many may also respond to different styles of teaching and explanations. An extreme grasshopper or inchworm may well be at risk of failure in maths, so knowing a learner's preferred thinking style can be very critical and essential information. This topic is dealt with in Chapter 4.

Attitude, anxiety and the affective domain

It would not be surprising if many clues for behaviours in this domain have not already been gathered. A few simple questions may boost these observations, such as,

'Do you like maths?'

'Do you think you are OK at doing maths?'

'Which bits of maths do you like best/worst?'

'Which bits do you think need some help?'

Look out for answers which suggest *permanent* attributes, such as 'I'm never going to be good at maths,' and *pervasive*, such as, 'I can't do fractions, I can't do any maths,' and *personal*, such as, 'I'm just hopeless at maths, none of my family can do maths.'

There is a maths anxiety scale, compiled in the USA in 1972 by Shuinn.[3]

Individual Education Plans (IEPs)

The work within this chapter can be the source of information for constructing IEP's. There are further resources in Appendix 5.

Always diagnosing

Any work set should have the potential to be diagnostic. Sadly this is not always so. Look at Figure 9.5 which was a worksheet set for my 13 year old daughter, who has a learning disability and at that time was functioning at Level 2. There are many criticisms one could level at this worksheet, but let's focus on the number content. It progresses quickly into very challenging decimal work, moves to a two step question by the third question and is more likely to generate the 'no answer' than any diagnosable errors. It is just not developmental enough to do a job.

Complete each triangle so the centre number is the sum of the corner number

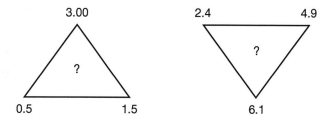

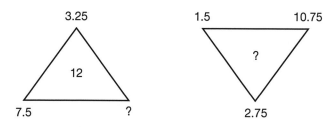

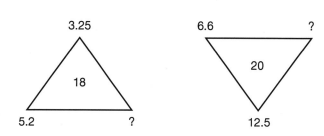

Figure 9.5 A non-diagnostic worksheet for a Level 2 pupil

To sum up

All work done by students provides diagnostic information, so in that sense diagnosis is ongoing, each new piece of work modifying the picture. If this appears to be too much of a task for a large class of children, then carefully constructed short tests can offer reasonable information on individuals and from the results for the whole group a useful diagnosis of your efforts as teacher or, if you need to rationalise, then a judgement on the curriculum!

Chapter 10

The nasties . . . long division and fractions

To illustrate some ideas for teaching maths topics I have picked long division and fractions. I would guess that the two leading contenders for the most anxiety inducing, no-attempt causing, high error rate topics in numeracy are these two topics, long division and fractions. I could speculate as to why this is so . . .

Long division

Long division by the traditional method (Figure 10.1) makes several demands. Let's do a task analysis.

Pupils need:

◆ multiplication facts for many numbers
◆ estimation skills
◆ sequencing skills
◆ organisation of work on paper
◆ subtraction skills
◆ understanding (Try to explain long division in terms of what is happening mathematically!)

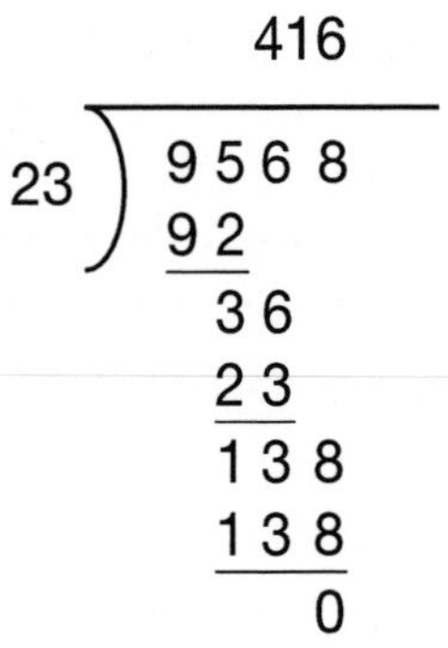

$$
\begin{array}{r}
416 \\
23 \overline{)\ 9\,5\,6\,8} \\
9\,2 \\
\hline
3\,6 \\
2\,3 \\
\hline
1\,3\,8 \\
1\,3\,8 \\
\hline
0
\end{array}
$$

Figure 10.1 'Traditional' long division

However if it has to be taught, try to decide which of the above factors is the most problematic for the pupil. As (almost) ever, ask the pupil to talk it through.

If it is the ability to work out the multiples, for example in 1139 ÷ 17, the pupil will need to know 6 × 17 and 7 × 17. This could be overcome by the setting up of a table of multiples. Set up the multiples in bold font first.

1 × 17 = 17	Encourage the use of inter-relationships. This
2 × 17 = 34	reduces the chance of cumulative errors.
3 × 17 = 51	
4 × 17 = 68	4 × 17 is twice 2 × 17
5 × 17 = 85	5 × 17 is half of 10 × 17
6 × 17 = 102	6 × 17 is 5 × 17 plus 17
7 × 17 = 119	7 × 17 is 5 × 17 plus 2 × 17 (85 + 34)
8 × 17 = 136	8 × 17 is 2 × 4 × 17
9 × 17 = 153	9 × 17 is 10 × 17 minus 17. Add the digits – they
10 × 17 = 170	should add up to 9 (1 + 5 + 3 = 9)

This table will then support the traditional algorithm (procedure).

If it is subtraction skills that are a problem, then use the interchange of operations, so

1139 ÷ 17 becomes y × 17 = 1139, that is
'What do I have to multiply 17 by to get 1139?'

Encourage initial estimating by looking at the values of the numbers and exploring possibilities, for example, try 17 × 10 = 170, which is much too small so move to 17 × 100 which is 1700, which is too big, but not that far away, so the answer should lie between 50 and 100.

Start with **50**

50 × 17 = 850

this is not enough so add on another **10** lots of 17 (170)

850 + 170 = 1020

another 10 lots of 17 will go beyond the target 1139 to 1190, so try **5** × 17 = 85

1020 + 85 = 1105

add on **2** more 17s to reach 1139

Add up all the added n × 17's   **50 + 10 + 5 + 2 = 67**

If this is set up without the explanations, it looks like:

$$50 \times 17 = 850$$
$$10 \times 17 = 170$$
$$\overline{1020}$$
$$10 \times 17 = 170$$
$$\overline{1190} \quad \text{(too big)}$$

(back one step) $60 \times 17 = 1020$
$$5 \times 17 = 85$$
$$\overline{1105}$$
$$2 \times 17 = 34$$
$$\overline{67 \times 17 = 1139}$$

If subtraction skills are not a problem, but the actual sequence of the traditional division procedure is the problem, either in terms of memory or spatial organisation, then a table of key value multipliers can be set up first:

$$1 \times 17 = 17$$
$$2 \times 17 = 34$$
$$4 \times 17 = 68$$
$$5 \times 17 = 85$$
$$10 \times 17 = 170 \qquad \text{then follow the pattern based on}$$
$$20 \times 17 = 10 \times 2 \times 17, \text{ etc.}$$

$$20 \times 17 = 340$$
$$40 \times 17 = 680$$
$$50 \times 17 = 850$$
$$100 \times 17 = 1700$$

Now divide by subtracting in (chunks) multiples of 17

$$1139$$
$$50 \times 17 \quad -850$$
$$\overline{289}$$
$$10 \times 17 \quad -170$$
$$\overline{119}$$
$$5 \times 17 \quad -85$$
$$\overline{34}$$
$$2 \times 17 \quad -34$$
$$\overline{67 \qquad 0}$$

The subtraction method above is close to the traditional algorithm for long division, but makes less spatial demands, is more logical and links division to repeated subtraction (or subtraction in chunks or partial products).

These methods also teach further understanding of numbers and number operations.

Remember that there is never a universal method. Teaching is about responding to the learner.

Adding and subtracting fractions

Let's start with a method that does not teach anything else except how to add and subtract fractions.

A functional approach to be used only as a last ditch strategy

When explanations of the finer points of fractions are failing and deep meaningful understanding is a distant goal and GCSEs are two terms away I go for the instrumental approach (and thus abandoning developmental principles and teaching for understanding). The methods are extreme inchworm.

The method involves classifying addition and subtraction of fractions into Types 1, 2 and 3. The focus is on the denominator, the bottom number of each fraction, asking the questions:

Are they the same?   Yes. Type 1

Is one a factor (or a multiple) of the other?   Yes. Type 2

Are they mathematically unrelated?   Yes. Type 3

(Note: Type 2 can be treated as a Type 3, but the answer will have to be simplified.)

Type 1: 'Same bottom line'

$$\text{e.g. } \frac{1}{5} + \frac{3}{5} = \frac{4}{5}$$

If the numbers on the bottom line (denominators, but how many pupils are going to remember that word) are the same, then you add (or subtract) the top numbers and the bottom numbers stay the same, hence reinforcing '*same* bottom line'.

Type 2: 'Goesinto'

$$\text{e.g. } \frac{1}{2} + \frac{1}{4} = \frac{3}{4} \qquad \frac{3}{20} + \frac{2}{5} = ?$$

Look at the bottom numbers – 2 goes into 4; and on the right 5 goes into 20. Both examples are Type 2. Thus the pupil needs to be able to know that one denominator is divisible by the other. If not move to Type 3.

So . . . if the bottom numbers of the fractions are divisible, do the division:

For example, $4 \div 2 = 2$ and $20 \div 5 = 4$

This gives the 'Goesinto number' and the fraction with the smaller value bottom number is multiplied by the 'Goesinto number'

$$\frac{1}{2} \times \frac{2}{2} = \frac{2}{4} \qquad \frac{2}{5} \times \frac{4}{4} = \frac{8}{20}$$

This now becomes a Type 1.

$$\frac{2}{4} + \frac{1}{4} = \frac{3}{4} \qquad \frac{3}{20} + \frac{8}{20} = \frac{11}{20}$$

The familiar $\frac{1}{2} + \frac{1}{4}$ example acts as a reminder of the Type 2 method.

Type 3: 'Doesn't Gointo'

In Type 3 fractions the two denominators (bottom numbers) are not multiples or factors of each other, for example:

$$\frac{2}{3} - \frac{2}{5} = \qquad \frac{3}{10} + \frac{5}{9} =$$

Appraisal of the bottom numbers shows that . . .

◆ 3 does not 'go into' 5 and 5 does not 'go into' 3
◆ 10 does not 'go into' 9 and 9 does not 'go into' 10

So these are Type 3 fraction problems (see Figure 10.2).

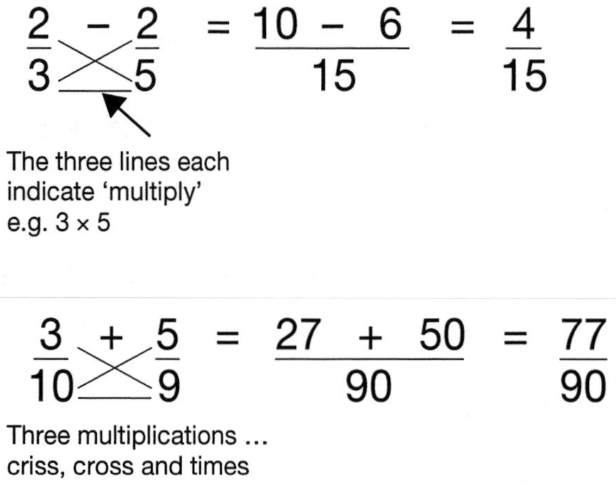

$$\frac{2}{3} \times \frac{2}{5} = \frac{10 - 6}{15} = \frac{4}{15}$$

The three lines each
indicate 'multiply'
e.g. 3×5

$$\frac{3}{10} + \frac{5}{9} = \frac{27 + 50}{90} = \frac{77}{90}$$

Three multiplications ...
criss, cross and times

Figure 10.2 The criss-cross-times method for fractions

The procedure is simple and involves multiplying (twice) diagonally across the + or − sign (criss-cross) and then multiplying the denominators (times).

The Types 1, 2 and 3 methods are purely mechanical, but do focus attention on the denominators. Type 3 has the benefit of a mnemonic (criss-cross-times). The labels also act as reminders to focus initially on the bottom number, the denominator.

Adding and subtracting fractions: a little more understanding

There are a number of misconceptions that handicap pupils' understanding of this topic. If the misconceptions are actively and positively acknowledged then the embedded problems they create may be pre-empted.

♦ There is a language and symbol factor in fractions. I asked a highly intelligent pupil 'What is half of fifty?' The almost instant answer was 'Twenty-five.' A little while later I presented the student with a sheet of paper on which I had written

$$\frac{1}{2} \times 50$$

She could not provide an answer, so I asked, 'Is the answer bigger or smaller than 50?' and she said 'Yes.' (See also Chapter 1.)

♦ There is a move away from previous experience where × meant getting a bigger answer. A new interpretation of multiplication is needed. I am always impressed by the fact that multiplications such as $\frac{2}{5} \times \frac{3}{7}$ give an answer that is smaller than either fraction. The rule is that when a multiplication is by a fraction which has a value of less than 1 the answer is smaller, so for $\frac{2}{5} \times \frac{3}{7}$, both fractions are less than 1 so the answer must be smaller than both $\frac{2}{5}$ and $\frac{3}{7}$.

♦ Another misconception (again language) is that a fraction is a single entity to be treated like any other number. Compare the vocabulary:

sixth, six   tenth, ten   two sevenths, twenty seven

The vocabulary is too similar to suggest there is any radical difference.

♦ Add and subtract has always applied to the numbers on each side of the sign + or −, so

$$4 + 6 = 10 \quad \text{and} \quad 16 - 9 = 7$$

The misconception is that this continues to be the case with fractions, that is, add means add and subtract means subtract, so mistakes are made, such as

$$\frac{1}{2} + \frac{1}{2} = \frac{2}{4} \qquad \frac{9}{10} - \frac{3}{7} = \frac{6}{3} \quad \text{and worse} \quad \frac{9}{10} - \frac{3}{10} = \frac{6}{0}$$

For fractions the + and − symbols now only apply selectively, that is to the top numbers (numerators).

◆   A particular value fraction may take many forms. The most common example is half, $\frac{1}{2}$. For an hour half is $\frac{30}{60}$. For a pound or a dollar or a Euro half is $\frac{50}{100}$. For a kilogram half is $\frac{500}{1000}$. For a year it is $\frac{6}{12}$ or $\frac{26}{52}$. For eggs it is $\frac{6}{12}$. For a day it is $\frac{12}{24}$. For a mile it is $\frac{880}{1760}$. And so on. Whilst pupils usually accept this for a half, it may be difficult for them to transfer that belief or concept or understanding to other fractions, such as a third or a seventh.

◆   This is a good example of the maths being easy until it has to be written down (as my friend and colleague Richard Ashcroft says). Asking 'What is a book plus a book?' is likely to elicit the answer, 'Two books.' followed by 'What is a ninth plus a ninth?' which then is likely to elicit the answer 'Two ninths', but $\frac{1}{9} + \frac{1}{9}$ presented as written symbols is likely to result in $\frac{2}{18}$.

Building the foundations

The first foundation is to understand why a fraction is written the way it is, that is two numbers, one on top of the other and separated by a line. A fraction could be visualised as incorporating a hidden division sign (Figure 10.3).

Figure 10.3 The hidden division sign

The golden rule of adding or subtracting fractions is that you can only start the addition or subtraction process when the fractions have been adjusted to have the same name (or denominator or bottom number). So, for example $\frac{1}{2} + \frac{1}{4}$ cannot be computated until the $\frac{1}{2}$ is renamed to be $\frac{2}{4}$, then

$$\frac{2}{4} + \frac{1}{4} = \frac{3}{4}$$

So students need to be able to rename fractions, understand what this means and why we do it. This is the second foundation.

Renaming implies that there already is a name. The name of $\frac{1}{2}$ is 'a half'. The name of $\frac{1}{7}$ is 'a seventh'. The name of $\frac{2}{5}$ is 'fifth' and there are two of them, hence 'two fifths'. So the name comes from the denominator, the bottom number, the number at the bottom of the fraction, the number below the dividing line.

As much time as is needed should be spent on developing the concept and skill of renaming. Renaming does what it says it does, it takes a fraction, for example one fifth, $\frac{1}{5}$, and gives it a new name, for example two tenths, $\frac{2}{10}$. It does *not* give it a new value. The new-named fraction must be an equivalent, same value, fraction. It remains the same value because it is multiplied by another fraction whose value is one (1), for example $\frac{2}{2}$. Examples can be taken from everyday experiences such as half an hour as $\frac{30}{60}$ ($\frac{1}{2} \times \frac{30}{30}$), half a pound (£) as $\frac{50}{100}$ ($\frac{1}{2} \times \frac{50}{50}$). The renaming fraction always has the same number as numerator and denominator (top number and bottom number) because it has a value of 1.

Tactile materials such as Cuisenaire rods, poker chips or stacker counters (from Crossbow Games, see Appendix p. 152) are good to show the equivalence of fractions. Folding squares or circles of paper can also illustrate the concept. The written symbols should always be shown alongside these concrete experiences.

Maybe it is worth using colours, one colour for the numerator and a different one for the denominator just to add focus to the fraction as having two number components. Or writing a big division sign ÷ on the board to remind learners that a fraction is a number divided by another number.

A problem could occur if learners have automatic recall of only a few number facts. This will handicap the extent of their ability to rename fractions, so this process will require a lot of carefully structured practice, with the focus on the process rather than on knowing all the basic facts.

A known or at least, a familiar example should be used as a first model, such as:

◆ $\frac{1}{2}$ to be renamed to have the same denominator as $\frac{1}{4}$;
◆ or $\frac{1}{3}$ to be renamed to have the same denominator as $\frac{1}{12}$ (using the familiar model of a clock again).

The overview/start up questions which should be asked are:

$$\text{For } \frac{1}{2} + \frac{1}{4}$$

◆ Do both fractions have to be renamed? Not if one denominator is a multiple of the other denominator. Four is a multiple of 2 so only the half has to be renamed.
◆ What number is used to change the chosen fraction, the half?

This number will be found by dividing the larger denominator (4) by the smaller denominator (2) which should give a whole number (2) and thereby avoiding creating a fraction within a fraction! In this example the renaming factor is therefore 2.

The top **and** bottom numbers of the fraction which has to be renamed have to be multiplied by this factor. In this example

$$\frac{1}{2} \times \frac{2}{2} = \frac{2}{4}$$

Thus the fraction remains the same value, it is still a half, but is renamed from being called *one half* to being called *two quarters*.

If both fractions have to be renamed, for example with $\frac{2}{3}$ and $\frac{1}{4}$ to have a common (meaning the same) denominator (meaning bottom number).

So in $\quad \dfrac{2}{3} + \dfrac{1}{4}$

- ◆ Both fractions have to be renamed.
- ◆ The simplest, but not necessarily the most numerically elegant, is to take the two denominators (bottom numbers) as factors of the new denominator and multiply them. So the new denominator becomes 3×4 and 4×3, that is 12.
- ◆ For renaming, the numerator (top number) and denominator *both* have to be multiplied.

So $\quad \dfrac{2}{3}$ is multiplied by $\dfrac{4}{4}$ to give $\dfrac{8}{12}$

and $\quad \dfrac{1}{4}$ is multiplied by $\dfrac{3}{3}$ to give $\dfrac{3}{12}$

Since both fractions are now renamed and written as twelfths they can now be added:

$$\dfrac{8}{12} + \dfrac{3}{12} = \dfrac{11}{12}$$

The answer $\frac{11}{12}$ is less than 1 and a sketch or estimate will show this to be as expected.

A circle picture as in Figure 10.4 can be used for estimates and appraisals of fraction sums. A clock is a good model (another reason to use an analogue watch) for $\frac{1}{2}$, $\frac{1}{3}$, $\frac{1}{4}$, $\frac{1}{6}$, $\frac{1}{12}$ and for inter-relating these fractions (Figure 10.5)

The process of 'mutual' renaming can be demonstrated with squares of paper. For example, the $\frac{2}{3}$ cannot be added to the $\frac{1}{4}$ because the fractions, the parts are not the same size (Figure 10.6). The first fraction, $\frac{2}{3}$, was created by dividing the square into three parts and using two of them. The second fraction, $\frac{1}{4}$, was created by dividing the square into four parts and using one of them.

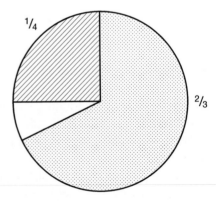

Figure 10.4 $\frac{1}{4} + \frac{2}{3}$

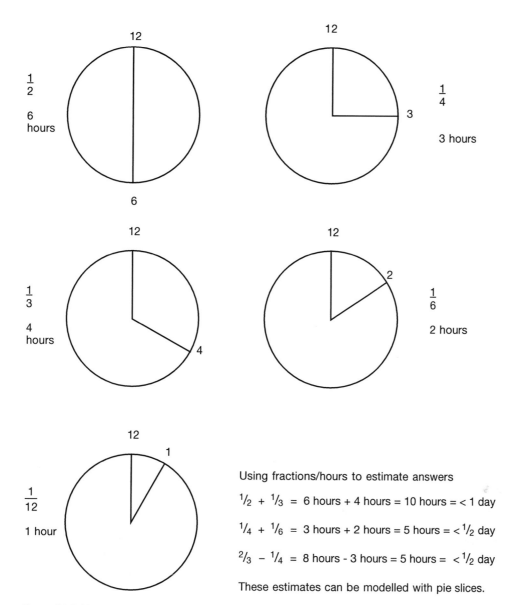

Using fractions/hours to estimate answers

$\frac{1}{2} + \frac{1}{3}$ = 6 hours + 4 hours = 10 hours = < 1 day

$\frac{1}{4} + \frac{1}{6}$ = 3 hours + 2 hours = 5 hours = < $\frac{1}{2}$ day

$\frac{2}{3} - \frac{1}{4}$ = 8 hours - 3 hours = 5 hours = < $\frac{1}{2}$ day

These estimates can be modelled with pie slices.

Figure 10.5 Fractions and clocks

To make both parts the same:

♦ the one divided into 3 parts initially is further divided, but into 4 parts (3 × 4 parts = 12 parts)
♦ the one divided into 4 parts initially is further divided, but into 3 parts (4 × 3 parts = 12 parts).

It's another example of the commutative property

$$a \times c = c \times a$$

and once again we return to the basic principles of numbers.

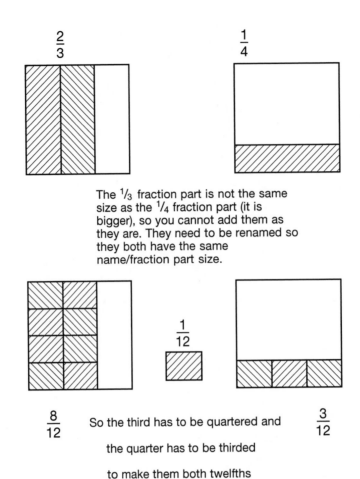

The ⅓ fraction part is not the same size as the ¼ fraction part (it is bigger), so you cannot add them as they are. They need to be renamed so they both have the same name/fraction part size.

So the third has to be quartered and

the quarter has to be thirded

to make them both twelfths

Both fractions have now had the same 'treatment', but in a different order.

The first original square was folded into thirds ($\frac{2}{3}$) and then into quarters ($\frac{1}{4}$).

The second original square was folded into quarters ($\frac{1}{4}$) and then into thirds ($\frac{2}{3}$).

Figure 10.6 Renaming fractions to make them have the same name

Multiplication of fractions

The use of the paper square above returns to the two dimensional model for multiplication. If you wanted to demonstrate $\frac{2}{3} \times \frac{3}{4}$, then a little paper folding could help.

First divide the paper into thirds and fold back to show $\frac{2}{3}$. Turn the paper through 90° and fold it into quarters and fold back to show $\frac{3}{4}$ of the $\frac{2}{3}$. Unfold to show the resulting area is $\frac{6}{12}$ (then show it is $\frac{1}{2}$ and thus smaller than either $\frac{3}{4}$ or $\frac{2}{3}$).

Or do this on acetate for an overhead projector, using premarked squares to help accuracy, or prepare a programme for Powerpoint.

To sum up

There is always more than one way to present information and to explain a maths topic. This chapter illustrates, for adding and subtracting fractions the extremes of a purely instrumental, procedure based method to a conceptual model based on the area theme which can be used so widely in many areas of basic numeracy. It also shows how methods for division can be adapted to match more closely the skills and deficits of the learner.

Appendix I

Further reading

Ashlock, R. B. (1998) *Error Patterns in Computation* 8th edn. Upper Saddle River, NJ. Merrill Prentice Hall.

Bley, N. and Thornton, C. (2001) *Teaching Mathematics to Students with Learning Disabilities* 4th edn. Austin, Texas: ProEd.

Butterworth, B. (1999) *The Mathematical Brain*. London, Papermac.

Chinn, S. (1998) *Sum Hope: Breaking the Numbers Barrier*. London, Souvenir Press.

Chinn, S. (2003) CD-ROM Version 3 *What to do When you Can't Learn the Times Tables*. Mark, Somerset, Markco Publishers.

Chinn, S.J. and Ashcroft, J.R. (1998) *Mathematics for Dyslexics: A Teaching Handbook* 2nd edn. London, Whurr.

Deboys, M. and Pitt, E. (1979) *Lines of Development in Primary Mathematics*. Belfast, Blackstaff Press.

Devlin, K. (2000) *The Maths Gene*. London, Weidenfeld and Nicolson.

Donlan, C. (ed.) (1998) *The Development of Mathematical Skills*. Hove, Psychology Press.

French, D., Connolly, W., Gardner, H., Hill, J., Jones, L., Marland, H. and Perks, P. (1992) *Mental Methods in Mathematics*. Leicester, Mathematical Association.

Geary, D. (1994) *Children's Mathematical Development*. Washington, DC, American Psychological Association.

Grauberg, E. (1998) *Elementary Mathematics and Language Difficulties*. London, Whurr.

Henderson, A. (1998) *Maths for the Dyslexic*. London, Fulton.

Kay, J. and Yeo, D. (2003) *Dyslexia and Mathematics*. London, Fulton.

Martin, H. (1996) *Multiple Intelligences in the Mathematics Classroom*. Arlington Heights, IL, IRI/Skylight Training.

Miles, T. and Miles, E. (eds) (2003) *Dyslexia and Mathematics* 2nd edn. London, RoutledgeFalmer.

Orton, A. (1999) *Patterns in the Teaching and Learning of Mathematics*. London, Cassell.

Thompson, I. (1999) *Issues in Teaching Numeracy in Primary Schools*. Buckingham, UK, OUP.

Yeo, D. (2002) *Dyslexia, Dyspraxia and Mathematics*. London, Whurr.

Checklists and resources

Checklist for choosing a textbook

◆ Is the level of maths difficulty suitable?
◆ Is the language level suitable?
◆ Is the language clear, unambiguous and concise?
◆ Are there diagrams which actually aid learning?
◆ Is the layout of the page clear and well spaced?
◆ Is there some 'real' maths content?
◆ Are the worked examples clearly, simply, concisely and flexibly explained?
◆ Are the exercises/questions presented clearly?
◆ Is the progression in difficulty in the exercises/questions smooth and without any quantum leaps?
◆ Can the exercises be easily modified for differentiation?
◆ Is key information highlighted?

Checklist for modifying a worksheet to differentiate for a student

A simple, informal diagnosis of the student will lead to suggestions for differentiation. For example reading accuracy and comprehension data will indicate the complexity of text which the student can access (but remember that maths has its own vocabulary and unique semantics).

◆ Are the items/questions accessible to a poor reader? Check by looking at the vocabulary and language levels.
◆ Are new and key words explained on the sheet or have they been explained when the sheet was handed out?
◆ Are the numbers used, in at least the first few questions, accessible, that is enough 1s, 2s, 5s whenever possible?
◆ Is there a quantum leap somewhere in the progression of difficulty?
◆ Are questions lined off to make them more distinct and less easy to mix up?
◆ Could diagrams be added to help the student's comprehension?

◆ Are there any examples to show how questions can be done and/or is there a summary of the main points tested in the questions?

◆ Have an appropriate number and range of questions been selected off the main worksheet?

◆ Can the layout be expanded so the student can answer on the worksheet (and thus eliminate copying and some writing)?

◆ Is it possible for the student to do and have marked the first two examples before taking the sheet away to attempt the remaining examples?

◆ Have you checked for pitfalls and pre-empted them? (Or do you want your student to fall???)

TEST PUBLISHERS AND SUPPLIERS

Ann Arbor
PO Box 1, Belford, Northumberland, NE70 7JX
tel 01668 214460 fax 01668 214484 e-mail enquiries@annarbor.co.uk

Crossbow Games
Crossbow Education, web site http://www.crossboweducation.com

Dyslexia Institute
Park House, Wick Road, Egham, Surrey, TW20 0HH
tel 01784 222300 fax 01784 222327 e-mail info@dyslexia-inst.org.uk

Hodder and Stoughton Educational
Bookpoint Ltd, Hodder and Stoughton Educational, Direct Services,
78 Milton Park, Abingdon, Oxon, OX14 4TD
tel 01235 827720 fax 01235 400454 e-mail orders@bookpoint.co.uk

Markco Publishing
Mark College, Mark, Highbridge, Somerset, TA9 4NP
tel 01278 641632 fax 01278 641426 e-mail post@markcollege.somerset.sch.uk

NFER-Nelson Education
Order processing: FREEPOST LON 16517, Swindon, SN2 8BR or fax 0845 601 5358 Customer Service tel 0845 602 1937 e-mail information@nfer-nelson.co.uk

Pro-Ed
8700 Shoal Creek Boulevard, Austin, Texas, TX 78758–9965, USA
tel 001 512 451 3246 fax 512 451 8542 web site http://www.proedinc.com

The Psychological Corporation
TPC Customer Services, Harcourt Education, Halley Court, Jordan Hill, Oxford, OX2 8EJ
tel 01865 888188 fax 01865 314 348 e-mail tpc@harcourteducation.co.uk

COLOURED OVERLAYS

I.O.O. Marketing Ltd, City University, London SE1 6DS
tel 020 7378 0330
e-mail admin@ioomarketing.co.uk

SUPPLIERS OF SOFTWARE

AVP, School Hill Centre, Chepstow, Monmouthshire, NP16 5PH
tel 01291 629 439
e-mail info@avp.co.uk web site http://www.avp.co.uk

Granada Learning, Granada Television, Quay Street, Manchester, M60 9EA
tel 0161 827 2927
e-mail info@granada-learning.com web site http://www.granada-learning.com/semercindex

Iansyst, Fen House, Fen Road, Cambridge, CB4 1UN
tel 01223 420 101
e-mail sales@dyslexic.com web site http://iansyst.co.uk
web site http://www.dyslexic.com

REM, Great Western House, Langport, Somerset, TA10 9YU.
tel 01458 254 700
e-mail info@r-e-m.co.uk web site http://www.r-e-m.co.uk

White Space, 41, Mall Road, London W6 9DG
tel 020 8748 5927
e-mail sales@wordshark.co.uk web site http://www.wordshark.co.uk

Evaluation questions for software

- Does it offer what you want, practice, learning, remedial intervention, extension or production (such as drawing graphs and charts)?
- Is it just a book on screen?
- Is the design cluttered?
- Is there mathematical structure?
- Is it just drill and kill?
- Does it irritate?
- Does it have voice output?
- How does it motivate, success and/or entertainment?
- Is it age specific in design?
- Does it address more than one way of learning?
- Is it good value for money?
- Can the learner use it independently?
- Does it have a record keeping system?
- Can the programme be individualised?
- Do users always have to start at the beginning or can they dip in at any point?
- Does it include assessment and/or diagnostic features?

Jog Your Memory cards for multiplication facts

2 × 7 = 14	5 × 7 = 35	2 × 8 = 16	5 × 8 = 40	1 × 8 = 8
2 × 6 = 12	5 × 6 = 30	1 × 6 = 6	1 × 7 = 7	Use the 'easy' nine to work out the 'tough' fourteen
Use two cards to work out one fact	HOW TO USE THE EASY NINE Example for 6 × 8 use two cards … use 5 × 8 = 40 and 1 × 8 = 8 to give 6 × 8 = 48 (which is also 8 × 6)	8 x 8 = 8×2×2×2 = 16 32 **64**	the 'tough' fourteen 6 × 6 6 × 7 7 × 6 6 × 8 8 × 6 7 × 7 7 × 8 8 × 7 3 × 6 6 × 3 3 × 7 7 × 3 3 × 8 8 × 3	
'jym' cards jog your memory cards		3x8 = 2x8 + 1x8 ≡ 8x3 6x8 = 5x8 + 1x8 ≡ 8x6 7x8 = 5x8 + 2x8 ≡ 8x7	3x6 = 2x6 + 1x6 ≡ 6x3 6x6 = 5x6 + 1x6 7x6 = 5x6 + 2x6 ≡ 6x7	3x7 = 2x7 + 1x7 ≡ 7x3 6x7 = 5x7 + 2x7 ≡ 7x6 7x7 = 5x7 + 2x7

$1 \times 2 = 2$ $2 \times 2 = 4$ $3 \times 2 = 6$ $4 \times 2 = 8$ $5 \times 2 = 10$ $6 \times 2 = 12$ $7 \times 2 = 14$ $8 \times 2 = 16$ $9 \times 2 = 18$ $10 \times 2 = 20$	**Using the first half of the 2× table to work out the second half**	2×2 $=$ 4
5×2 $=$ 10	1×2 $=$ 2	3×2 $=$ 6
4×2 $=$ 8	$6 = 5 + 1$ $7 = 5 + 2$ $8 = 5 + 3$ $9 = 5 + 4$ **Use two cards to work out one fact**	**Examples:** $6 \times 2 = 5 \times 2 + 1 \times 2$ $\quad\quad = 10 + 2 =$ 12 $8 \times 2 = 5 \times 2 + 3 \times 2$ $\quad\quad = 10 + 6 =$ 16 $9 \times 2 = 5 \times 2 + 4 \times 2$ $\quad\quad = 10 + 8 =$ 18 Now work out 7×2

7 / **5 + 2**	**6** / **5 + 1**	**3** / **2 + 1**
4 / **2 × 2**	**9** / **10 − 1**	**8** / **2 × 2 × 2** / **10 − 2**
The links **3 = 2 + 1** **4 = 2 × 2** **6 = 5 + 1** **7 = 5 + 2** **8 = 2 × 2 × 2** **9 = 10 − 1**	**Linking the 'hard' numbers to the 'easy' numbers.**	

1 × 2 = 2	1 × 10 = 10	1 × 5 = 10 5
2 × 2 = 4	2 × 10 = 20	2 × 5 = 20 10
3 × 2 = 6	3 × 10 = 30	3 × 5 = 30 15
4 × 2 = 8	4 × 10 = 40	4 × 5 = 40 20
5 × 2 = 10	5 × 10 = 50	5 × 5 = 50 25
6 × 2 = 12	6 × 10 = 60	6 × 5 = 60 30
7 × 2 = 14	7 × 10 = 70	7 × 5 = 70 35
8 × 2 = 16	8 × 10 = 80	8 × 5 = 80 40
9 × 2 = 18	9 × 10 = 90	9 × 5 = 90 45
10 × 2 = 20	10 × 10 = 100	10 × 5 = 100 50

1 × 9 = 10 9	2 × 1 = 2	5 × 1 = 5
2 × 9 = 20 18	2 × 2 = 4	5 × 2 = 10
3 × 9 = 30 27	2 × 3 = 6	5 × 3 = 15
4 × 9 = 40 36	2 × 4 = 8	2 × 4 = 20
5 × 9 = 50 45	2 × 5 = 10	5 × 5 = 25
6 × 9 = 60 54	2 × 6 = 12	5 × 6 = 30
7 × 9 = 70 63	2 × 7 = 14	5 × 7 = 35
8 × 9 = 80 72	2 × 8 = 16	5 × 8 = 40
9 × 9 = 90 81	2 × 9 = 18	5 × 9 = 45
10 × 9 = 90	2 × 10 = 20	5 × 10 = 50

THE ' EASY' TABLES	REMEMBER	
1 ×	THE ORDER OF MULTIPLYING CAN BE SWAPPED	
2 ×	examples:	
5 ×	4 x 6 = 6 x 4	
	8 x 7 = 7 x 8	
10 ×	3 x 9 = 9 x 3	

Appendix 4

Setting an inclusive maths department policy

General principles

All work must be modified appropriately to enable included pupils to succeed and achieve the maximum levels of which they are capable. Proactive intervention could be seen to be at three broad levels:

1 Simple adjustments to lessons which include giving instructions that will not overload poor short term memory, repetition of instructions (aural) reinforced by board work (visual).
2 More directed intervention which might include seating a pupil where he can see the board clearly, hear and see the teacher properly, basic modifications to written material, for example selecting fewer examples for the pupil to complete, checking early on in individual work to ensure he has started and is doing the work correctly.
3 Individual intervention which may include a specially modified worksheet, using a bigger font, different coloured paper, using a learning support assistant who has been briefed on how to intervene for the topic being taught.

To achieve the goal of maximising the success of the included special needs child or the uncertain learner (who may never carry a label) the following factors will be acknowledged and positive adjustments will be made to all teaching.

Consistency

Insecure learners like as much of the structure and arrangements around lessons to be as consistent as is possible. For example, in a mental arithmetic session, set a pattern of asking the child a question, so the question does not catch him unawares. Perhaps flag up the question, ask another pupil another question and then return to re-ask the question. Perhaps ask a part question. Make your strategy a routine.

Multisensory and developmental work

There are several reasons why work needs to be presented in a multisensory way and with a developmental structure.

◆ Some pupils always need to start with the concrete and can then move to the symbolic and on to the abstract. It is usually better if the materials chosen to represent the concept have consistency (see above), for example, the area model.
◆ Some pupils are visual learners.
◆ Work should always be developmental to give slower learners the best chance of reducing the performance gap. This includes referring the current topic back to an earlier level and checking on the foundations of the topic. This also acts as revision and review.

Language factors

Although it may seem to be stating the obvious, language must be kept clear and simple. This is not just the 'louder and slower' technique, but an intellectual appraisal of the vocabulary and sentence structures used in instruction. This includes dealing with new vocabulary and any dual meaning vocabulary, such as 'take away' for 'subtraction'.

Presentation issues, spoken and written

The factors that the learner brings to presentation by the teacher are short term memory, pragmatic language skills and reading skills. The teacher can accommodate these as far as is possible in the structure of the lesson, including clear and uncluttered board work, and straightforward clear language that sticks to the point.

Safe learning and risk

Learners must feel safe to ask questions and know they will not be ridiculed (even mildly) and feel safe to make a start on questions, even though their initial work may be very wide of the best procedure.

Pupil involvement and interactions

Insecure learners may quietly withdraw mentally from lessons, just sitting unobtrusively at the back of the class. They need to be drawn, empathetically, into the lesson. Quiet pupils deserve as much attention as the noisy pupils.

Structured for revisions, reviews and recaps

The curriculum must be structured for revision. Any extension of a previously studied topic must be preceded by a review of the work so far and then summarised at the end of the lesson. (Remember that old adage, 'Tell them what you are going to teach, teach it and tell them what you have just taught.')

Structured for success

Genuine success is a motivating influence. Work should be structured and presented in small steps that encourage success and do not suddenly face learners with insurmountable hurdles (but don't forget this approach may need to be modified for grasshoppers). This requires a lot of checking of all work given to pupils. Assuming that an exercise is suitable without actually working it through is not acceptable.

Relevant

Whenever possible, the work must be shown to be relevant. Building in relevance is a good subject for departmental discussions.

Speed and pace

It is important to remember that the speed at which pupils do maths may be yet another example of normal distribution. It would be educationally immoral to ignore either extreme of that distribution. This applies to both mental arithmetic and written problems.

Empathetic teaching

This could be the only consideration in that it summarises all the others. Empathy implies an understanding of the learner and all that he brings to a lesson, from attitude and anxiety to mathematical memory to problem solving skills and pro-actively acknowledging those attributes in the way you teach.

Responsive

Many modern teaching schemes for numeracy encourage children to explore different methods of solving problems. This acknowledges that the most appropriate method for an individual pupil may be individual to that pupil. Teaching should be responsive to the learner and the way he learns and thinks, his attitude and interests, which implies that teachers must be aware of the way each learner learns and what he, the learner, brings to each lesson.

Learning and thinking styles

Following on from responsive teaching is a need to be aware of the learning styles and the thinking styles of each pupil in each classroom, in particular those pupils whose thinking styles are at the extremes of the continuum.

Marking, feedback and praise

Learners' attributions will be influenced by the feedback they receive in lessons, whether it is verbal or written comments used in marked work. Dramatic use of red pens is banned, indeed any red marking is banned. Try discrete marking in green.

Check new work early

Before an error pattern is internalised by the learner.

Teach patterns

Do not assume that all learners will automatically 'discover' the pattern, idea or concept that you, the teacher are so artfully guiding them towards. Sometimes it is best to know the final destination in order to appreciate the route taken.

Finally,

Do not assume . . .

It may also be a good exercise for a Mathematics Department to set up its own key principles of teaching mathematics, for example:

BASIC PRINCIPLES OF TEACHING MATHEMATICS

Vocabulary

Make sure that *all* vocabulary is understood and placed in a mathematical context, e.g. 'take away' means 'subtract' in mathematics.

Language

Mathematics has its own language. It is not just the ability to read the words, but the ability to comprehend the maths meaning, for example, 'Remove the brackets' $(y + 3)(y - 5)$ is not meant literally. Ensure the pupil is focused on the mathematical meaning.

The big picture and details

Grasshoppers will appreciate the outline of the whole picture, but need to learn to notice detail and to document their methods. Inchworms need to learn to overview and see the big picture. Putting the concept into a 'real' situation and linking the maths to previous experiences benefits both thinking styles.

Relate to other maths topics

Revise and build. (This includes taking every opportunity to reinforce number skills.)

Easy numbers

Use the 'easy' numbers to illustrate the first worked examples and in the first practise of independent examples. Focus on the concept, not on the number facts.

Quick check

Mark the first two practise examples before allowing further progress so the learner's error patterns do not become embedded in memory.

Speed

Remember that some pupils take longer to do work, so select fewer examples for them, but make sure these still cover the range of necessary experience (and look out for quantum leaps that occur in some sets of questions, where, for example, questions 1, 2 and 3 are straightforward and then, wham, question 4 leaps to degree level).

Remember also that some pupils retrieve and process information more slowly, so make allowances for that.

Criterion referenced tests

These tests may be used for pre- and post-testing or for following up diagnostic clues from other tests, such as examinations or standardised tests.

Obviously, it is easy to make further tests or to modify these, but, for a busy teacher, here are a few 'I made earlier'.

The tests can be used to give a simple measure of progress or the individual items can provide more information by showing which critieria are met or failed. An analysis of the errors the pupil made can take the information obtained to a deeper level. Like all tests, it depends what and how much the teacher needs to know.

The tests can also be used to set up a maths Individual Education Plan (IEP) by identifying targets at both the very specific micro level (improve skills for adding two digit numbers to two digit numbers) or a broader, more macro level (improve whole number addition skills).

Later in this Appendix there are some tests for estimation skills. Again, these can be used as they are or modified to suit a particular need. Estimation skills often give a better indicator of number sense, which again can be a source of information for IEPs.

ADDITION – WHOLE NUMBER

There are two parallel tests, which may be used for:

◆   Pre- and post-testing, using the complete tests;
◆   Providing a second example when a subject gets an item wrong. The second example can be used to confirm if an error pattern exists. Single examples may be chosen;
◆   Progress on the specified criteria.

The addition items test:

1   Single digit plus single digit, total under 20.
2   Two digit plus one digit with carrying.
3   Two digit plus two digit, carrying in units column.
4   Two digit plus two digit, carrying in units and tens columns.
5   Three digit plus three digit, carrying in units column, zero in tens.
6   Four digit plus four digit, carrying in units column, zero in hundreds column.

These criteria enable the teacher to identify specific areas of achievement and weakness.

This information may well link to information obtained from observations of other tests and work. For example, an extreme reliance on procedure may well link with a dominant inchworm thinking style. Errors due to poor basic fact knowledge could well be a consequence of poor retrieval from memory of basic facts or may show that the fact knowledge is insecure when used in problems rather than just straight recall.

ADDITION – whole number		ADDITION – whole number	
name .... date		name .... date	
1a 7 + 6 =	2a 17 + 8 =	1b 6 + 8 =	2b 24 + 7 =

3a   36
      +47
      ‾‾‾
	4a 64
	      +78
	      ‾‾‾
		3b 58
		      +35
		      ‾‾‾
			4b 47
			      +86
			      ‾‾‾

5a   209
      +481
      ‾‾‾
	6a 3058
	    +5436
	    ‾‾‾
		5b 677
		      +103
		      ‾‾‾
			6b 4062
			    +3329
			    ‾‾‾

SUBTRACTION – WHOLE NUMBER

There are two parallel tests, which may be used for:

◆ Pre- and post-testing, using the complete tests;
◆ Providing a second example when a subject gets an item wrong. The second example can be used to confirm if an error pattern exists. Single examples may be chosen;
◆ Progress on the specified criteria.

The subtraction items test:

1 Two digit minus single digit, no borrowing/decomposing/trading.
2 Two digit minus one digit with borrowing/decomposing/trading.
3 Two digit plus two digit, carrying in units column.
4 Three digit minus two digit, borrowing/decomposing/trading in units and tens columns.
5 Three digit minus three digit, borrowing/decomposing/trading in units column, zero in tens.
6 Four digit minus four digit, borrowing/decomposing/trading in units column, zero in tens and hundreds column.

These criteria enable the teacher to identify specific areas of achievement and weakness.

This information may well link to information obtained from observations of other tests and work. For example, an extreme reliance on procedure may well link with a dominant inchworm thinking style. Errors due to poor basic fact knowledge could well confirm poor retrieval skills or may show that the fact knowledge is insecure when used in problems rather than just straight recall.
   Procedural errors may include problems with zero.

SUBTRACTION – whole number	
name .... date	
1a $18 - 6 =$	2a $26 - 7 =$
3a $\begin{array}{r} 84 \\ -47 \\ \hline \end{array}$	4a $\begin{array}{r} 142 \\ -66 \\ \hline \end{array}$
5a $\begin{array}{r} 703 \\ -226 \\ \hline \end{array}$	6a $\begin{array}{r} 9001 \\ -2049 \\ \hline \end{array}$

SUBTRACTION – whole number	
name .... date	
1b $19 - 4 =$	2b $24 - 8 =$
3b $\begin{array}{r} 76 \\ -28 \\ \hline \end{array}$	4b $\begin{array}{r} 134 \\ -88 \\ \hline \end{array}$
5b $\begin{array}{r} 605 \\ -348 \\ \hline \end{array}$	6b $\begin{array}{r} 8004 \\ -1056 \\ \hline \end{array}$

MULTIPLICATION – WHOLE NUMBER

There are two parallel tests, which may be used for:

◆ Pre- and post-testing, using the complete tests;
◆ Providing a second example when a subject gets an item wrong. The second example can be used to confirm if an error pattern exists. Single examples may be chosen;
◆ Progress on the specified criteria.

Note that 'easy' times table facts have been used. This section is testing procedures, not times table knowledge.
  The multiplication items test:

1 Single digit times single digit.
2 Two digit times single digit.
3 Two partial products which may be combined to answer the third part.
4 Two digit times two digit, digit values below 5.
5 Three digit times two digit, two digit numbers using only 2 and 1.
6 Three digit times three digit, low numerals used in both numbers. Zero in multiplier.

(Note that 'difficult' times table facts have not been used so that multiplication skills, rather than basic fact skills are the focus of the tests.)

MULTIPLICATION – whole number

name ....   date ....

1a $2 \times 6 =$ **2a** $20 \times 6 =$

3a $5 \times 7 =$ $10 \times 7 =$ $15 \times 7 =$

4a $14 \times 23 =$ **5a** $179 \times 21 =$

6a $213 \times 105 =$

MULTIPLICATION – whole number

name ....   date ....

1b $2 \times 8 =$ **2b** $20 \times 8 =$

3b $5 \times 8 =$ $10 \times 8 =$ $15 \times 8 =$

4b $13 \times 24 =$ **5b** $268 \times 22 =$

6b $123 \times 102 =$

These criteria enable the teacher to identify specific areas of achievement and weakness.

This information may well link to information obtained from observations from other tests and work. For example, an extreme reliance on procedure may well link with a dominant inchworm thinking style. Errors due to poor basic fact knowledge could well confirm slow and inaccurate retrieval of the basic facts or may show that basic fact knowledge is insecure when used in problems rather than just straight recall. The student may not be able to organise the partial products on paper, failing to line them up in place values, or forgetting to multiply by 10 as well as 2 when multiplying by 20. This may be due to a lack of understanding of the procedure or poor organisation when writing numbers.

DIVISION – WHOLE NUMBER

There are two parallel tests (see p. 168), which may be used for:

(see p. 168)

◆ Pre- and post-testing, using the complete tests;
◆ Providing a second example when a subject gets an item wrong. The second example can be used to confirm if an error pattern exists. Single examples may be chosen;
◆ Progress on the specified criteria.

Note that 'easy' basic division facts have been used. This section is testing procedures, not times table knowledge, which is tested in Section 1.

The division items test:

1 Two digit divided by single digit, no carrying.
2 Two digit divided by single digit, carrying.
3 Two digit divided by single digit, with carrying and remainder (decimal /fraction).
4 Four digit number divided by ten, no remainder.
5 Three digit divided by 'easy' two digit, no remainder.
6 Four digit divided by 'hard' two digit, no remainder.

These criteria enable the teacher to identify specific areas of achievement and weakness.

This information may well link to information obtained from observations of other tests and work. For example, an extreme reliance on procedure may well link with a dominant inchworm thinking style, though the division procedure is difficult to comprehend. Poor basic fact knowledge will handicap the process. The least problematic consequence of this being slower work.

Division is often perceived as an almost mystical process and may well be done purely as a rote exercise. It is likely that some pupils will just not start the work as they simply have none of the skills needed to do this complex procedure.

It may be informative to ask the pupil for an estimated answer, or if they can see a link to multiplication (for example for question 5b: 'What would I have to multiply 15 by to get 765?')

DIVISION – whole number

name ....   date ....

1a $16 \div 2$	2a $58 \div 2$
3a $2\overline{)77}$	4a $10\overline{)5030}$
5a $15\overline{)660}$	6a $48\overline{)1536}$

DIVISION – whole number

name ....   date ....

1b $35 \div 5$	2b $72 \div 2 =$
3b $2\overline{)57}$	4b $10\overline{)7010}$
5b $15\overline{)765}$	6b $52\overline{)1768}$

ADDITION – DECIMAL

There are two parallel tests (see p. 169), which may be used for:

◆ pre- and post-testing, using the complete tests;
◆ providing a second example when a subject gets an item wrong. The second example can be used to confirm if an error pattern exists. Single examples may be chosen;
◆ progress on the specified criteria.

The addition items test:

1 Units, tenths plus units, tenths with carrying in tenths.
2 Units, tenths, hundredths plus units, tenths, hundredths with carrying in tenths and hundredths.
3 Tens, units, tenths plus units, no carrying.
4 Tenths, hundredths plus units.
5 Units, tenths, hundredths, thousandths plus tens, units, tenths, hundredths, thousandths, carrying in thousandths and hundredths.
6 Units, tenths, hundredths, thousandths plus units, tenths, hundredths, carrying in hundredths and tenths.

These criteria enable the teacher to identify specific areas of achievement and weakness.

Errors may well confirm information from other sources. For example, lining up from left or right without acknowledging the decimal point may show perseverance from work with whole numbers and a lack of awareness of the significance of the decimal point and its relevance to place values.

ADDITION – decimal

name .... date ....

1a $2.3 + 4.8$ 2a $4.26 + 3.87$

3a $14.6 + 3$ 4a $0.72 + 4$

5a $13.001 + 2.899$ 6a $3.678 + 8.35$

ADDITION – decimal

name .... date ....

1b $5.9 + 3.4$ 2b $6.79 + 1.54$

3b $15.2 + 4$ 4b $0.64 + 3$

5b $1.798 + 12.002$ 6b $4.756 + 7.26$

SUBTRACTION – DECIMAL

There are two parallel tests, which may be used for:

◆ Pre- and post-testing, using the complete tests;
◆ Providing a second example when a subject gets an item wrong. The second example can be used to confirm if an error pattern exists. Single examples may be chosen;
◆ Progress on the specified criteria.

The subtraction items test:

1 Tens, units, tenths minus units, tenths with no borrowing/decomposing/trading.
2 Tens, units, tenths, hundredths minus units, tenths, hundredths with borrowing/ decomposing/trading in tenths column.
3 Tens, units, tenths minus units, no borrowing/decomposing/trading.

4   Unit minus tenths with borrowing/decomposing/trading.
5   Tens, units, tenths, hundredths, thousandths minus units, tenths, hundredths, thousandths, borrowing/decomposing/trading in thousandths, hundredths and tenths.
6   Tens, units, tenths, hundredths, thousandths minus units, tenths, hundredths, borrowing/decomposing/trading in hundredths, tenths and units.

These criteria enable the teacher to identify specific areas of achievement and weakness.

Lining up from left or right without acknowledging the decimal point may show perseverance from work with whole numbers and a lack of awareness of the significance of the decimal point.

It could be that the results for subtraction are poorer than those for addition of decimal numbers. Sometimes the extra step of a decimal point as well as a subtraction is an overload.

There could be more 'no answers' showing an insecure grasp of the principles of decimal numbers.

SUBTRACTION – decimal

name ....   date ....

1a 14.6 − 2.5   2a 24.26 − 3.44

3a 14.6 − 3   4a 5 − 0.8

5a 13.231 − 1. 444   6a 22.008 − 8.72

SUBTRACTION – decimal

name ....   date ....

1b 15.9 − 3.4   2b 15.29 − 1.54

3b 15.2 − 4   4b 8 − 0.6

5b 15.121 − 1.666   6b 24.006 − 7.24

FRACTIONS

There are two parallel tests, which may be used for:

◆ Pre- and post-testing, using the complete tests;
◆ Providing a second example when a subject gets an item wrong. The second example can be used to confirm if an error pattern exists. Single examples may be chosen;
◆ Progress on the specified criteria.

The fraction items test:

1 Addition of two fractions with the same denominator.
2 Subtraction of two fractions with the same denominator.
3 Addition of two fractions where one denominator is a factor of the other.
4 Subtraction of two fractions where one denominator is a factor of the other.
5 Addition of two fractions where the denominators are not factors or multiples.
6 Subtraction of two fractions where the denominators are not factors or multiples.
7 Multiplication of two fractions.
8 Multiplication of two fractions. (Ask if the answer will be same value, smaller, bigger.)

These criteria enable the teacher to specify specific areas of achievement and weakness.

Does the subject know that multiplication with fractions can make answers smaller? Can the subject estimate an answer, even if just at the 'bigger than 1', 'smaller than 1' level? If the pupil adds all these questions it may indicate that he does not appreciate the different signs or that he just rushed through. Simple questioning could determine which was the reason. If it was just a matter of rushing, allow the pupil to attempt the questions again, pointing out which operation is required for each question.

FRACTIONS

name ....

1a $\dfrac{1}{5} + \dfrac{2}{5} =$

2a $\dfrac{3}{7} - \dfrac{2}{7} =$

3a $\dfrac{2}{3} + \dfrac{1}{6} =$

4a $\dfrac{7}{8} - \dfrac{3}{4} =$

5a $\dfrac{2}{5} + \dfrac{2}{7} =$

6a $\dfrac{3}{4} - \dfrac{2}{3} =$

7a $\dfrac{3}{4} \times \dfrac{3}{5} =$

8a $\dfrac{5}{7} \times \dfrac{9}{10} =$

FRACTIONS   name ....

1b $\dfrac{2}{9} + \dfrac{4}{9} =$ **2b** $\dfrac{9}{11} - \dfrac{7}{11} =$

3b $\dfrac{1}{2} + \dfrac{3}{8} =$ **4b** $\dfrac{7}{10} - \dfrac{2}{5} =$

5b $\dfrac{1+3}{3} + \dfrac{3}{7} =$ **6b** $\dfrac{4}{5} - \dfrac{5}{8} =$

7b $\dfrac{2}{3} \times \dfrac{7}{11} =$ **8b** $\dfrac{2}{5} \times \dfrac{3}{8} =$

ORALLY PRESENTED TEST FOR ESTIMATION

There are two parallel versions of the oral test, which may be used for:

◆   Pre- and post-testing, using the complete tests;
◆   Providing a second example when a subject gets an item wrong. The second example can be used to confirm if an error pattern exists. Single examples may be chosen.

Remind the subject that for estimation an approximate answer, a good guess is all that is needed. This section is read to the subject.

After the test is completed ask the subject to explain how he/she did each question. Prompt if necessary ('Did you change the value of 94 to something else? What did you chose?')

Ask if they saw any connection between the two parts of Question 3.

ORALLY PRESENTED TEST FOR ESTIMATION

Make and use printed cards for each question

1a **What is an easier number to use instead of 96 if you are estimating an answer to this addition sum?**

   96 + 434

2a **Estimate the total cost of this shopping bill** (show bill)

   £1.95   47p   £9.99   56p   88p   £1.12

3a **Estimate the product (answer) to these multiplication sums**

   21 × 96   52 × 18

4a **Estimate how many chocca bars at 35p each you can buy for £4**

5a **Estimate the answer to this division sum**

   55.32 ÷ 0.489

ESTIMATION

Use the estimation cards for each question

1b **What is an easier number to use instead of 94 if you are estimating an answer to this addition sum?**

   657 + 94

2b **Estimate the total cost of this shopping bill**

   45p   £9.99   58p   81p   £2.95   £1.20

3b **Estimate the product (answer) to these multiplication sums**

   22 × 95   51 × 19

4b **Estimate how many yuffee bars at 26p each you can buy for £5**

5b **Estimate the answer to this division sum**

   52.73 ÷ 0.487

WRITTEN ESTIMATION TEST FOR ARITHMETIC

name .... date ....

ADDITION

1) $38 + 28$
3) $12.3 + 7.8$
5) $63 + 12.05$

2) $308 + 89$
4) $19.09 + 10.91$

SUBTRACTION

1) $67 - 38$
3) $843 - 648$
5) $37.6 - 4$

2) $172 - 96$
4) $601 - 346$
6) $21.003 - 2.114$

MULTIPLICATION

1) 9×32
3) 4.9×12.4

2) 49×22
4) 91×982

DIVISION

1) $48.2 \div 1.94$

2) $788 \div 15$

WRITTEN ESTIMATION TEST FOR ARITHMETIC

There is one version of a written estimation test for arithmetic. As when investigating thinking style, ask the subject 'How did you do that?' This will be the key diagnostic question. For example, $788 \div 15$ might be estimated by rounding 788 to 800 and 15 to 16. There are 100 eights in 800, so there will be 50 sixteens. Another possibility is to start with 15, double to 30, double again to 60 then add one more 15 to make 75, or just multiply 15 by 5 to show there are approximately five fifteens in 78, and so approximately fifty in 788.

Although both tests are looking at estimation skills, they also lead to information on how numbers are understood and manipulated and thus they investigate the pupil's understanding of the four operations and basic facts.

Notes

1 Introduction: learning difficulties in mathematics

1   V.A. Krutetskii, *The Psychology of Mathematical Abilities in Schoolchildren*, Chicago, University of Chicago Press, 1976.
2   R.R. Skemp, *The Psychology of Learning Mathematics*, London, Penguin, 1986, pp. 64, 78.
3   B. Butterworth, *The Dyscalculia Screener*, London, NFER-Nelson, 2003.
4   A front page article in the *Times* of 30/12/02 headed 'Exam stress strikes seven-year-olds' claims that the Key Stage 1 tests are causing symptoms of excessive anxiety including loss of appetite, insomnia, bed-wetting, forgetfulness and depression. These are our children!

3 What the curriculum asks pupils to do and where difficulties may occur

1   For further details of methods for teaching addition and subtraction see S. Chinn, *What to do When you Can't Add and Subtract*, Baldock, Herts, Egon, 1999.

4 Thinking styles in mathematics

1   M.R. Marolda and P.S. Davidson, 'Mathematical learning styles and differentiated teaching strategies', *Perspectives*, 26, 3, pp. 10–15, 2000.
2   See S.J. Chinn, *The Test of Thinking Style in Mathematics*, Mark, Somerset, Markco Publishing, 2003.
3   CASE. Cognitive Acceleration in Science Education. See P. Adey, M. Shayer and C. Yates, *Thinking Science* 2nd edn, Cheltenham, Nelson Thornes, 1994.
4   CAME. Cognitive Acceleration in Mathematics Education. See M. Adhami, D.C. Johnson and M. Shayer, *Thinking Maths: The Programme for Accelerated Learning in Mathematics*, Oxford, Heinemann Educational, 1998.

5 Developmental perspectives

1   R. Gagne, *The Conditions of Learning*, New York, Holt, Rinehart & Winston, 1970.

6 The language of maths

1 See A. Henderson and E. Miles, *Basic Topics in Mathematics for Dyslexics*, London, Whurr, 2001.

8 The inconsistencies of maths

1 R.R. Skemp, *The Psychology of Learning Mathematics* 2nd edn, Harmondsworth, Pelican, 1986.
2 G.T. Buswell and C.M. Judd *Summary of Educational Investigations Relating to Arithmetic: Supplementary Educational Monographs*, Chicago, University of Chicago Press.

9 Assessment and diagnosis

1 N. France, *The Profile of Mathematical Skills*, Windsor, NFER-Nelson, 1979.
2 J.M. Engelhardt, 'Analysis of children's computational errors: a qualitative approach', *British Journal of Educational Psychology*, 47, pp. 149–54, 1977.
3 Shuinn, as described in Alexander, L. and Murray, C. 'The development of an abbreviated version of the Mathematics Anxiety Rating Scale', *Measurement and Evaluation in Counseling and Development*, vol. 22 pp. 143–50, 1989.

Index

eBooks – at www.eBookstore.tandf.co.uk

A library at your fingertips!

eBooks are electronic versions of printed books. You can store them on your PC/laptop or browse them online.

They have advantages for anyone needing rapid access to a wide variety of published, copyright information.

eBooks can help your research by enabling you to bookmark chapters, annotate text and use instant searches to find specific words or phrases. Several eBook files would fit on even a small laptop or PDA.

NEW: Save money by eSubscribing: cheap, online access to any eBook for as long as you need it.

Annual subscription packages

We now offer special low-cost bulk subscriptions to packages of eBooks in certain subject areas. These are available to libraries or to individuals.

For more information please contact webmaster.ebooks@tandf.co.uk

We're continually developing the eBook concept, so keep up to date by visiting the website.

www.eBookstore.tandf.co.uk